CREATED TO BELIEVE

60 DAYS OF FAITH, STRENGTH, AND PURPOSE

RICHARD "REASON" GARRETT

Liberated Publishing Inc.

1725 Wilma Rudolph Blvd Suite J

Clarksville, TN 37040

Copyright © 2011 Richard "Reason" Garrett.

All rights reserved. No part of this book may be reproduced in any form or by any means without the prior written consent of the Publisher, excepting brief quotes used in reviews.

If you purchased this book without a cover, you should be aware that this book is stolen property. It was reported as "unsold and destroyed" to the Publisher and neither the Author nor the Publisher has received any payment for this "stripped book".

ISBN: 979-8-9986057-0-3

First Printing: December 2011

Printed in the United States of America

Dedication

To every soul who's ever questioned their worth,
wondered if they were enough,
or felt too broken to be used by God—
this is for you.

May these pages remind you that you were created on purpose,
for a purpose,
and with a purpose.

And to my family, friends, and faith community—
thank you for believing in me,
even when I struggled to believe in myself.

This devotional is a piece of my journey.
May it inspire yours.

—Richard "Reason" Garrett

My greatest blessing and biggest inspiration—my family

Foreword
by Laquvia Garrett

Over the years, I've come to understand that some of the hardest battles we face aren't the ones people see—they're the silent ones within. The tension between who we are and who we're becoming. The fight between faith and fear, clarity and confusion, strength and exhaustion.

And if we're honest, many of us have wrestled with questions like, Am I enough? Can I really do this? Does God even see me?

That's why this devotional means so much to me—because it speaks directly to those questions with honesty, wisdom, and hope.

Created to Believe was birthed from my husband's own journey—through seasons of uncertainty, breakthroughs, quiet resilience, and God's undeniable grace. I've watched Richard pour his heart into this devotional, not from a pedestal of perfection, but from the path of progress. His story, like yours and mine, is still unfolding. And that's exactly what makes this 60-day journey so impactful.

Each day you'll discover truth grounded in Scripture, real-life parables that bring spiritual lessons to life, and heartfelt prayers to guide you. Whether you're at a crossroads, in a comeback season, or just trying to stay faithful day by day—this devotional will meet you right where you are.

It's not just a book to read. It's a journey to walk. A mirror to reflect. A tool to grow.

I truly believe that you were not created to live stuck, silent, or small. You were created for something greater. You were created to believe.

Let these next 60 days draw you closer to the God who sees you, knows you, and still has incredible purpose for your life.

With love and belief in your journey,
—Laquvia Garrett

Table of Contents

Dedication 5

Foreword 6

Day 1: Trusting God's Timing 13

Day 2: Walking in Purpose 16

Day 3: Faithful in the Small Things 20

Day 4: Finding Strength in Weakness 24

Day 5: Victory Through Christ 28

Day 6: The Joy of Serving 32

Day 7: The Peace of God 36

Day 8: Hope in God 40

Day 9: God's Promises Never Fail 44

Day 10: God's Love Never Fails 48

Day 11: God's Grace Is Sufficient 52

Day 12: Walking in God's Strength 56

Day 13: Overcoming Fear Through Faith 60

Day 14: Unpacking Bitterness 64

Day 15: God's Guidance in Uncertainty 68

Day 16: God's Presence in the Storm 72

Day 17: God's Faithfulness in Every Season 77

Day 18: The Strength of Community 80

Day 19: The Joy of Obedience 84

Day 20: God's Faithfulness in Trials 89

Day 21: Walking in Faith 92

Day 22: God's Comfort in Times of Grief 96

Day 23: God's Joy in Every Circumstance 100

Day 24: God's Protection in Uncertainty 104

Day 25: The Strength of Patience 108

Day 26: God's Provision in Every Need 112

Day 27: God's Peace in Chaos 116

Day 28: God's Wisdom for Life's Decisions 120

Day 29: The Courage to Trust God 125

Day 30: God's Strength in Our Weakness 128

Day 31: Soaring After the Storm 132

Day 32: The Light of God's Word 136

Day 33: God's Power in Prayer 140

Day 34: Strength of Perseverance 144

Day 35: God's Love as Our Foundation 148

Day 36: God's Purpose in Every Season 152

Day 37: The Power of Forgiveness 156

Day 38: Living with Purpose 160

Day 39: The Power of Faithfulness 164

Day 40: The Power of Generosity 168

Day 41: God's Peace in Waiting 172

Day 42: The Beauty of Humility 176

Day 43: The Gift of Contentment 180

Day 44: God's Strength in Community 184

Day 45: The Power of Gratitude 189

Day 46: The Strength of Integrity 192

Day 47: The Power of Perseverance 196

Day 48: The Beauty of Compassion 200

Day 49: The Blessing of Rest 204

Day 50: The Gift of Hope 208

Day 51: The Power of Faith 213

Day 52: The Power of Kindness 216

Day 53: The Gift of Patience 220

Day 54: The Strength of Self-Control 224

Day 55: The Power of Obedience 228

Day 56: The Power of Encouragement 232

Day 57: Replenished Through Serving 236

Day 58: The Gift of Generational Legacy 240

Day 59: The Power of Vision 244

Day 60: The Journey of Faith 248

Acknowledgments 253

About the Author 255

Day 1: Trusting God's Timing

God's Perfect Plan

God's timing often doesn't align with ours, but His plan is always perfect. Ecclesiastes 3:1 reminds us, "To everything there is a season, a time for every purpose under heaven." Trusting His timing requires patience and faith, even when the path ahead is unclear.

Isaiah 40:31 reassures us, "But those who wait on the Lord shall renew their strength; they shall mount up with wings like eagles, they shall run and not be weary, they shall walk and not faint." Waiting is not a passive act but an opportunity to grow in trust and reliance on God.

Parable: The Farmer and the Bamboo

There once was a farmer who planted a grove of bamboo seeds, expecting to see growth quickly. He watered the ground every day and waited. Months passed, then years, but nothing sprouted. Friends mocked him, calling him foolish for wasting his time.

Despite the ridicule, the farmer kept watering and nurturing the soil. Then, in the fifth year, the bamboo suddenly shot up—growing over 80 feet in just six weeks. What the farmer knew was that during those seemingly barren years, the bamboo was growing strong roots underground, preparing for its rapid ascent.

In the same way, God often works beneath the surface, strengthening our foundation before revealing His plans. Trusting His timing means believing that He is preparing us for growth and blessings we cannot yet see.

Trusting God in the Waiting

Waiting seasons often test our patience, but they also build our character. Romans 8:28 assures us, "And we know that all things work together for good to those who love God, to those who are the called according to His purpose." Trusting God means believing that He is working behind the scenes, even when we don't see immediate results.

Joseph's story is a powerful reminder of this truth. Betrayed by his brothers, sold into slavery, and imprisoned unfairly, Joseph could have felt abandoned. Yet, in God's perfect timing, he was elevated to a position of leadership, saving countless lives. Genesis 50:20 reflects his faith: "But as for you, you meant evil against me; but God meant it for good."

Reflection Questions

What areas of your life require you to trust God's timing more fully?

_____

_____

_____

How has God's timing in past situations revealed His faithfulness?

_____

_____

_____

How can you use waiting seasons to grow in faith and reliance on Him?

_____

_____

_____

Prayer Prompt

Lord, thank You for the assurance that Your timing is perfect. Teach me to trust in Your plans, even when they don't align with mine. Help me to grow in patience and faith, knowing that You are always working for my good. Amen.

Day 2: Walking in Purpose

God's Unique Calling

Each of us was created with a unique purpose that only we can fulfill. Jeremiah 29:11 assures us, "For I know the thoughts that I think toward you, says the Lord, thoughts of peace and not of evil, to give you a future and a hope." Walking in purpose means aligning our lives with God's will and trusting that He has equipped us for the journey.

Romans 12:6-8 reminds us, "Having then gifts differing according to the grace that is given to us, let us use them." God's purpose for our lives is often revealed through the gifts and passions He has placed within us.

Parable: The Violinist in the Subway

A renowned violinist, dressed in casual clothes, once played at a busy subway station during rush hour. Thousands of commuters passed him by, barely noticing the extraordinary music. Only a few stopped to listen, and even fewer recognized him. What they didn't know was that this same violinist had performed in sold-out concert halls worldwide, with tickets costing hundreds of dollars.

The violinist was the same; the setting was different. In much the same way, walking in purpose isn't always about the platform—it's about using our God-given talents, no matter where we are. When we trust God's purpose for our lives, we can make an impact, whether we're on a grand stage or in the humblest of circumstances.

Aligning with God's Purpose

Discovering and walking in purpose often requires obedience and courage. Jesus called Peter to leave his fishing nets and follow Him, saying, "Follow Me, and I will make you fishers of men" (Matthew 4:19 NKJV). Peter's willingness to abandon his livelihood for God's calling led to a purpose far greater than he could have imagined.

Living in purpose also means trusting that God's timing is perfect. Moses spent 40 years as a shepherd before God called him to lead His people out of Egypt. Purpose unfolds as we take steps of faith, trusting that God will guide us along the way.

Reflection Questions

What gifts or talents has God given you to fulfill His purpose in your life?

_____

_____

_____

How can you step out in faith to walk in the calling God has placed on your heart?

_____

_____

_____

In what ways can you trust God's timing as you pursue your purpose?

_____

_____

_____

Prayer Prompt

Lord, thank You for the unique purpose You have for my life. Help me to recognize and use the gifts You've given me, no matter the setting or platform. Teach me to trust in Your timing and to walk boldly in obedience to Your calling. Amen.

Day 3: Faithful in the Small Things

The Value of Small Acts

God often uses the small, unseen acts of faithfulness to prepare us for greater opportunities. Jesus said, "He who is faithful in what is least is faithful also in much" (Luke 16:10 NKJV). Faithfulness in the small things reflects the condition of our hearts and our willingness to honor God in all we do.

Colossians 3:23 encourages, "And whatever you do, do it heartily, as to the Lord and not to men." When we approach even the smallest tasks with excellence and devotion, God sees and rewards our faithfulness.

Parable: The Hidden Bricklayer

In the construction of a great cathedral, three bricklayers were asked about their work. The first said, "I'm laying bricks." The second replied, "I'm building a wall." But the third, with a gleam in his eye, said, "I'm constructing a house of worship where generations will come to seek God."

Though each man was performing the same task, their perspectives revealed their sense of purpose. Years later, when the cathedral was complete, it was the third bricklayer—who had remained faithful in his humble work—that the townspeople remembered for his vision and joy.

Similarly, God calls us to approach every task, no matter how small, with the mindset that it contributes to His greater plan. When we are faithful in the little things, we partner with Him in building something eternal.

Small Acts, Big Impact

Throughout Scripture, God honors those who are faithful in the small things. David tended his father's sheep with care, never knowing that this humble responsibility was preparing him to lead a nation as king. Ruth faithfully gleaned in the fields, and her diligence led her to Boaz and ultimately into the lineage of Christ.

Faithfulness in small tasks positions us for greater blessings. Matthew 25:21 reflects this truth: "Well done, good and faithful servant; you were faithful over a few things, I will make you ruler over many things. Enter into the joy of your lord."

Reflection Questions

What small responsibilities or tasks in your life can you approach with more faithfulness?

_____

_____

_____

How can you shift your perspective to see the eternal significance of your daily work?

_____

_____

_____

In what ways has God used your faithfulness in small things to open doors for greater opportunities?

_____

_____

_____

Prayer Prompt

Lord, thank You for the opportunities to serve You in the small things. Help me to approach every task with a heart of faithfulness and a mindset of purpose. Teach me to trust that even the smallest acts of obedience contribute to Your greater plan. Amen

Day 4: Finding Strength in Weakness

God's Power in Our Weakness

Weakness is not a limitation in God's eyes—it is an opportunity for His strength to be revealed. Paul writes, "And He said to me, 'My grace is sufficient for you, for My strength is made perfect in weakness'" (2 Corinthians 12:9 NKJV). When we admit our dependence on God, He fills the gaps with His power and grace.

Isaiah 40:29 assures us, "He gives power to the weak, and to those who have no might He increases strength." Trusting God in our weakest moments allows Him to work mightily in ways we cannot.

Parable: The Cracked Pot

A servant carried water every day to his master's house using two pots suspended on a pole. One pot was flawless, while the other was cracked, leaking water along the path. For years, the cracked pot felt ashamed of its flaw, believing it was of little use.

One day, the servant said to the cracked pot, "Do you notice the flowers growing along your side of the path? I planted seeds there, and every day, your leaks have watered them. Without you, this beauty wouldn't exist."

The pot's perceived weakness was actually its greatest contribution. Similarly, our weaknesses often become the very areas where God's glory shines the brightest, nurturing life and beauty in ways we may not see at first.

Strength Through Surrender

When we surrender our weaknesses to God, He transforms them into strengths. Moses doubted his ability to lead Israel out of Egypt, citing his lack of eloquence. Yet God used Moses' humility and dependence on Him to deliver an entire nation (Exodus 4:10-12).

Jesus Himself embraced weakness on the cross, allowing Himself to be vulnerable to fulfill God's redemptive plan. His resurrection demonstrates that what appears weak to the world is powerful in God's hands.

Reflection Questions

What weaknesses in your life have you struggled to accept or embrace?

_____

_____

_____

How can you invite God to use those weaknesses for His glory?

_____

_____

_____

What examples in your own life show how God's strength has worked through your limitations?

_____

_____

_____

Prayer Prompt

Lord, thank You for reminding me that my weaknesses are not obstacles to You. Teach me to surrender my flaws and limitations, trusting that Your power is made perfect in my weakness. Help me to walk in confidence, knowing that You work through my life for Your glory. Amen.

Day 5: Victory Through Christ

Our Source of Victory

Victory in life is not about our strength or efforts—it is found in Christ alone. 1 Corinthians 15:57 reminds us, "But thanks be to God, who gives us the victory through our Lord Jesus Christ." Through His death and resurrection, Jesus overcame sin, death, and every challenge we face.

John 16:33 provides comfort: "In the world you will have tribulation; but be of good cheer, I have overcome the world." This assurance allows us to face life's trials with courage, knowing that the ultimate victory has already been won.

Parable: The Marathon Runner

A young man trained for months to run his first marathon. On race day, everything went wrong. At mile 10, his legs cramped; by mile 20, he felt like giving up. But then he noticed something in the distance—a man in his 70s, running steadily, smiling as he encouraged others along the way.

The young man asked the older runner how he managed to stay so calm and focused. The man replied, "The victory isn't at the finish line—it's in knowing I'm running the race the best I can with the strength I've been given."

Inspired, the young man pushed through his pain and completed the race. Like the older runner, we must remember that victory in Christ isn't just about crossing the finish line—it's about relying on His strength every step of the way.

Living as Overcomers

As believers, we are more than conquerors through Christ. Romans 8:37 declares, "Yet in all these things we are more than conquerors through Him who loved us." Walking in victory means standing on God's promises and trusting His power to overcome fear, doubt, and adversity.

Victory also requires perseverance. Hebrews 12:1-2 encourages, "Let us run with endurance the race that is set before us, looking unto Jesus, the author and finisher of our faith." Fixing our eyes on Jesus helps us endure and claim the victory He has already secured.

Reflection Questions

What challenges in your life require you to rely on Christ's victory instead of your own strength?

_____

_____

_____

How can you shift your focus from the finish line to trusting God's strength in the journey?

_____

_____

_____

In what ways can you encourage others to live as overcomers through Christ?

_____

_____

_____

Prayer Prompt

Lord, thank You for the victory You have secured for me through Christ. Teach me to trust in Your power and to walk confidently in the promises of Your Word. Help me to persevere through life's challenges with faith, knowing that You are my source of strength and triumph. Amen.

Day 6: The Joy of Serving

Serving as an Act of Worship

Serving others is a reflection of God's love and an act of worship. Jesus said, "The Son of Man did not come to be served, but to serve, and to give His life as a ransom for many" (Matthew 20:28 NKJV). When we serve, we follow His example and bring glory to God.

Colossians 3:23 encourages, "And whatever you do, do it heartily, as to the Lord and not to men." Serving with a heart of humility and joy transforms even the simplest acts into opportunities to honor God.

Parable: The Town's Unsung Hero

In a small town, there was a man named Victor who quietly cleaned the local park every morning. No one knew who he was, but the park was always spotless, the flowers watered, and the benches freshly painted. Over time, the park became a haven for families, a place where children laughed and friendships flourished.

One day, a group of residents discovered Victor at work and asked him why he put so much effort into something no one seemed to notice. He replied, "This park isn't just a park—it's a gift to the town. When I care for it, I'm serving God by bringing joy to others."

Victor's quiet dedication exemplifies the joy of serving. Like him, when we serve with love and purpose, we create ripples of impact that glorify God and uplift others.

Finding Purpose in Service

God designed us to serve as part of His kingdom. Ephesians 2:10 reminds us, "For we are His workmanship, created in Christ Jesus for good works, which God prepared beforehand that we should walk in them." Serving others allows us to live out our faith and fulfill the purpose God has placed in our lives.

Jesus demonstrated the ultimate act of service by washing His disciples' feet, saying, "I have given you an example, that you should do as I have done to you" (John 13:15 NKJV). Serving with humility and love reflects Christ's heart.

Reflection Questions

How can you find joy in serving others, even in small ways?

_____

_____

_____

What gifts or resources has God given you to serve your community?

_____

_____

_____

How does serving others deepen your relationship with God and reflect His love?

_____

_____

_____

Prayer Prompt

Lord, thank You for the opportunity to serve others as an act of worship. Teach me to serve with humility, joy, and purpose, knowing that my actions reflect Your love. Help me to use my gifts to make a positive impact and to bring glory to Your name. Amen.

Day 7: The Peace of God

Experiencing True Peace

Peace is one of God's greatest gifts, offering comfort and assurance regardless of our circumstances. Jesus said, "Peace I leave with you, My peace I give to you; not as the world gives do I give to you. Let not your heart be troubled, neither let it be afraid" (John 14:27 NKJV). True peace comes from trusting in God's presence and promises.

Isaiah 26:3 assures us, "You will keep him in perfect peace, whose mind is stayed on You, because he trusts in You." By fixing our hearts and minds on God, we experience the calm that transcends understanding.

Parable: The Sleeping Sailor

A ship once sailed through a ferocious storm, with towering waves battering its sides and the crew panicking as the vessel swayed violently. Amid the chaos, one sailor slept soundly in his bunk. When asked how he could remain so calm, he replied, "I trust the captain. He's navigated storms like this before, and I know he'll guide us safely to shore."

The sailor's trust in the captain mirrors the peace we find when we trust God with our lives. While storms may rage around us, peace is possible when we rest in the knowledge that God is in control.

Peace in the Storms

Life's challenges often test our sense of peace, but God's presence sustains us. When Jesus calmed the storm, He asked His disciples, "Why are you so fearful? How is it that you have no faith?" (Mark 4:40 NKJV). Faith in God shifts our focus from our circumstances to His sovereignty.

Paul's words in Philippians 4:6-7 offer a blueprint for finding peace: "Be anxious for nothing, but in everything by prayer and supplication, with thanksgiving, let your requests be made known to God; and the peace of God, which surpasses all understanding, will guard your hearts and minds through Christ Jesus."

Guarding Your Peace

Maintaining God's peace requires intentionality. Colossians 3:15 instructs, "And let the peace of God rule in your hearts." Spending time in prayer, worship, and Scripture strengthens our trust in Him, helping us guard our hearts against worry and fear.

Jesus' words in John 16:33 offer hope: "In the world you will have tribulation; but be of good cheer, I have overcome the world." Through Him, we can experience unshakable peace, even in uncertain times.

Reflection Questions

What storms in your life are threatening to disrupt your peace?

_____

_____

_____

How can prayer and trust in God help you experience peace in challenging circumstances?

_____
_____
_____

In what ways can you guard your heart and mind to maintain God's peace daily?

_____
_____
_____

Prayer Prompt

Lord, thank You for the peace that only You can provide. Help me to trust in Your promises and to fix my heart and mind on You, even in the midst of life's storms. Teach me to guard my peace and to rest in the assurance of Your presence. Amen.

Day 8: Hope in God

The Anchor for Our Souls

Hope is the anchor that keeps us steady in the storms of life. Hebrews 6:19 describes hope as "an anchor of the soul, both sure and steadfast." This hope is not based on our circumstances but on the unchanging character and promises of God.

Jeremiah 29:11 reassures us, "For I know the thoughts that I think toward you, says the Lord, thoughts of peace and not of evil, to give you a future and a hope." God's plans are always for our good, even when we cannot see the full picture.

Parable: The Village Well

In a drought-stricken village, the only source of water was an old well. Every day, villagers came with their empty buckets, trusting that the well would provide enough for their needs. Over time, the well's water level fluctuated, sometimes rising high and other times dipping low. But no matter what, the well never ran dry.

One villager observed, "The well isn't full every day, but it always has enough to sustain us. Its strength lies in what we cannot see—its deep, hidden source."

Like the well, our hope in God is sustained by the unseen. Though our circumstances may fluctuate, God's faithfulness runs deep, providing exactly what we need at the right time.

Hope in the Waiting

Waiting on God often tests our hope, but it also strengthens it. Isaiah 40:31 encourages, "But those who wait on the Lord shall renew their strength; they shall mount up with wings like eagles, they shall run and not be weary, they shall walk and not faint." Hope allows us to trust God's timing, knowing that He is always working for our good.

Abraham's journey illustrates this truth. Despite his old age, he held onto God's promise of a son. Romans 4:20-21 says, "He did not waver at the promise of God through unbelief, but was strengthened in faith, giving glory to God, and being fully convinced that what He had promised He was also able to perform."

Eternal Hope

Our ultimate hope lies in the promise of eternal life with God. Paul writes, "For I consider that the sufferings of this present time are not worthy to be compared with the glory which shall be revealed in us" (Romans 8:18). This eternal perspective reminds us that our present struggles are temporary and that God's promises will never fail.

Jesus Himself assures us of this hope, saying, "In My Father's house are many mansions… I go to prepare a place for you" (John 14:2 NKJV). The promise of eternity gives us the strength to endure and persevere.

Reflection Questions

How can you anchor your hope in God rather than in temporary circumstances?

_____

_____

_____

In what areas of your life are you waiting on God, and how can you trust His timing?

_____

_____

_____

How does the promise of eternity shape your perspective on present challenges?

_____

_____

_____

Prayer Prompt

Lord, thank You for being the anchor of my soul and the source of my hope. Teach me to trust in Your promises, even in times of waiting. Help me to focus on the eternal hope You provide and to live with confidence in Your faithfulness. Amen.

Day 9: God's Promises Never Fail

Standing on God's Word

God's promises are the foundation of our faith. Numbers 23:19 declares, "God is not a man, that He should lie, nor a son of man, that He should repent. Has He said, and will He not do? Or has He spoken, and will He not make it good?" Unlike human promises, God's Word is unchanging and trustworthy.

Joshua 21:45 reminds us, "Not a word failed of any good thing which the Lord had spoken to the house of Israel. All came to pass." Trusting in God's promises gives us strength and assurance, even in uncertain times.

Parable: The Old Lighthouse

An old lighthouse stood tall on a rocky shore, its light guiding ships safely through treacherous waters. Over the years, storms battered the lighthouse, and its exterior showed signs of wear. Yet the light within never wavered, faithfully shining through every storm.

When asked how it endured, the lighthouse keeper explained, "The strength of the lighthouse isn't in its walls but in its foundation and the unwavering light inside."

Like the lighthouse, God's promises are a steady foundation in the storms of life. Though circumstances may try to shake us, His Word remains a beacon of hope and guidance.

Faith in the Waiting

God's promises often require patience and faith. Abraham waited 25 years for the fulfillment of God's promise of a son, yet he held onto his faith. Romans 4:21 says, "And being fully convinced that what He had promised He was also able to perform." Trusting in God's timing helps us remain steadfast, even when the wait feels long.

The Israelites, too, experienced God's faithfulness as they entered the Promised Land. Though the journey was fraught with challenges, every promise God made to them was fulfilled. Their story reminds us that God's timing is perfect, and His promises never fail.

Claiming God's Promises

To experience the fullness of God's promises, we must claim them through prayer and faith. Jesus said, "If you abide in Me, and My words abide in you, you will ask what you desire, and it shall be done for you" (John 15:7 NKJV). Abiding in God's Word strengthens our faith and aligns our hearts with His will.

Speaking and declaring God's promises over our lives helps us stay grounded in His truth. Jeremiah 1:12 assures us, "I am watching to see that My word is fulfilled" (NIV). God is faithful to honor His Word, and He invites us to stand firm in His promises.

Reflection Questions

What promises from God are you holding onto in this season?

_____

_____

_____

How can you deepen your faith as you wait for God's promises to unfold?

_____

_____

_____

In what ways can you claim and declare God's promises over your life?

_____

_____

_____

Prayer Prompt

Lord, thank You for the assurance that Your promises never fail. Teach me to trust in Your Word and to stand firm in faith, even when the waiting feels long. Help me to abide in Your truth and to declare Your promises with confidence. Amen.

Day 10: God's Love Never Fails

The Depth of God's Love

God's love is unchanging, unconditional, and eternal. Romans 8:38-39 declares, "For I am persuaded that neither death nor life, nor angels nor principalities nor powers, nor things present nor things to come, nor height nor depth, nor any other created thing, shall be able to separate us from the love of God which is in Christ Jesus our Lord."

This love is not based on our performance or worthiness but flows from the very nature of who God is. 1 John 4:8 simply states, "God is love." Resting in this truth gives us peace and security, knowing we are deeply loved by our Creator.

Parable: The Prodigal Daughter

A young woman named Clara left home to pursue a life of freedom and independence. She distanced herself from her family, chasing dreams that ultimately left her feeling empty and broken. When her life hit rock bottom, she hesitated to return home, ashamed of her mistakes.

One day, she mustered the courage to call her father. Before she could finish apologizing, he interrupted with tears in his voice: "Clara, I've been waiting for you every day. Come home. There's nothing you've done that could ever make me stop loving you."

God's love for us is like that of Clara's father—always waiting, always welcoming, no matter how far we stray. His love never fails, and He rejoices when we return to Him.

Love in Action

God's love is not passive; it is active and sacrificial. John 3:16 reminds us, "For God so loved the world that He gave His only begotten Son, that whoever believes in Him should not perish but have everlasting life." Jesus' sacrifice on the cross is the ultimate demonstration of this love.

We are called to reflect God's love in our own lives. Jesus said, "A new commandment I give to you, that you love one another; as I have loved you, that you also love one another" (John 13:34 NKJV). Loving others unconditionally and sacrificially is one of the greatest ways to show God's love to the world.

The Transforming Power of Love

God's love has the power to heal, restore, and transform. 2 Corinthians 5:17 declares, "If anyone is in Christ, he is a new creation; old things have passed away; behold, all things have become new." Embracing God's love frees us from shame and fear, giving us a new identity in Him.

Living in God's love also helps us extend grace and forgiveness to others. 1 John 4:18 reminds us, "There is no fear in love; but perfect love casts out fear." His love allows us to walk in confidence, knowing that we are deeply valued and cared for.

Reflection Questions

How does understanding God's unconditional love change the way you view yourself and others?

_____
_____
_____

In what areas of your life do you need to trust more fully in God's love?

_____
_____
_____

How can you reflect God's love to others in practical ways?

_____
_____
_____

Prayer Prompt

Lord, thank You for Your unfailing love that reaches every part of my life. Help me to rest in the truth of Your love and to reflect it to others through my actions and words. Teach me to love unconditionally, as You have loved me. Amen.

Day 11: God's Grace Is Sufficient

The Gift of Grace

God's grace is an unmerited gift, given freely and abundantly. Ephesians 2:8-9 reminds us, "For by grace you have been saved through faith, and that not of yourselves; it is the gift of God, not of works, lest anyone should boast." This grace not only saves us but sustains us in every season of life.

Paul reflected on God's sustaining grace when he wrote, "But by the grace of God I am what I am, and His grace toward me was not in vain" (1 Corinthians 15:10 NKJV). Grace empowers us to live purposefully, relying not on our strength but on God's.

Parable: The Broken Clay Vase

A master potter crafted a beautiful clay vase, but during a storm, the vase fell and cracked. Heartbroken, the owner considered discarding it. Instead, the potter collected gold powder and carefully filled the cracks, creating a dazzling, unique design. What once seemed ruined now became more beautiful and valuable.

The vase's transformation reflects God's grace in our lives. Even in our brokenness, God's grace fills the gaps, creating something more beautiful than we can imagine. His grace doesn't discard—it restores, making us a masterpiece for His glory.

Grace in Weakness

God's grace shines brightest in our moments of weakness. Paul shares his personal experience in 2 Corinthians 12:9: "And He said to me, 'My grace is sufficient for you, for My strength is made perfect in weakness.'" When we embrace our need for God, His power is revealed in our lives.

Weakness is not a limitation but an opportunity for God to work through us. Gideon's army was reduced to a small, unlikely group, yet by God's grace, they achieved victory over their enemies (Judges 7:2-7). God's strength, not human ability, brings success.

Extending Grace to Others

As recipients of God's grace, we are called to extend it to others. Colossians 3:13 encourages, "Bear with each other and forgive one another if any of you has a grievance against someone. Forgive as the Lord forgave you." Showing grace reflects God's love and creates opportunities for healing and reconciliation.

Grace in action might involve forgiving a friend, being patient with a difficult colleague, or offering help to someone in need. By extending grace, we reflect the heart of Christ and create a ripple effect of kindness and compassion.

Reflection Questions

How has God's grace sustained you in moments of weakness or failure?

_____

_____

_____

What areas of your life need more reliance on God's grace rather than your own strength?

_____

_____

_____

How can you show grace to others in your daily interactions?

_____

_____

_____

Prayer Prompt

Lord, thank You for Your all-sufficient grace that carries me through every challenge. Teach me to embrace my weakness and rely on Your strength. Help me to extend grace to others, reflecting the love and forgiveness You have shown me. Amen.

Day 12: Walking in God's Strength

Strength Beyond Ourselves

Life often brings challenges that feel overwhelming, but God promises to be our source of strength. Isaiah 41:10 reassures us, "Fear not, for I am with you; be not dismayed, for I am your God. I will strengthen you, yes, I will help you, I will uphold you with My righteous right hand." His strength sustains us when our own abilities fall short.

Paul echoes this truth in Philippians 4:13: "I can do all things through Christ who strengthens me." Trusting in God's power allows us to face life's trials with courage and endurance.

Parable: The Widow's Jar of Oil

A poor widow was on the verge of losing everything when the prophet Elisha asked her, "What do you have in the house?" She replied, "Nothing but a jar of oil." Elisha instructed her to gather empty vessels from her neighbors and pour the oil into them.

Though it seemed impossible, as the widow poured, the oil miraculously multiplied until every vessel was filled. What seemed small and insufficient in her hands became abundant through God's power.

Like the widow, we often feel we have little to offer. Yet when we trust God and step out in faith, His strength multiplies our efforts, accomplishing far more than we could on our own.

Strength in Weakness

God's strength is often most evident in our weakness. 2 Corinthians 12:9 reminds us, "My grace is sufficient for you, for My strength is made perfect in weakness." Surrendering our struggles and limitations to God allows His power to work through us.

David's victory over Goliath is a powerful example. Armed with just a sling and five stones, David defeated a giant not because of his own strength but because he trusted in God's power (1 Samuel 17:45-50). His faith reminds us that God's strength is greater than any obstacle we face.

Drawing Strength Daily

To walk in God's strength, we must stay connected to Him. Jesus said, "Abide in Me, and I in you. As the branch cannot bear fruit of itself unless it abides in the vine, neither can you, unless you abide in Me" (John 15:4 NKJV). Through prayer, worship, and studying His Word, we draw on His power to navigate life's challenges.

Isaiah 40:31 encourages us, "But those who wait on the Lord shall renew their strength; they shall mount up with wings like eagles, they shall run and not be weary, they shall walk and not faint." Renewing our strength daily allows us to persevere with faith and confidence.

Reflection Questions

In what areas of your life are you relying on your own strength instead of God's?

_____

_____

_____

How can you trust God to multiply what you have, even if it feels small or insufficient?

_____

_____

_____

What practices can help you stay connected to God's strength every day?

_____

_____

_____

Prayer Prompt

Lord, thank You for being my source of strength in every situation. Help me to trust in Your power and to surrender my weaknesses to You. Teach me to rely on You daily, knowing that Your strength is sufficient for every need. Amen.

Day 13: Overcoming Fear Through Faith

God's Assurance in Fear

Fear can paralyze us, but God's Word offers assurance and courage. Isaiah 41:13 reminds us, "For I, the Lord your God, will hold your right hand, saying to you, 'Fear not, I will help you.'" God's presence and promises give us the strength to face our fears and move forward in faith.

Paul writes in 2 Timothy 1:7, "For God has not given us a spirit of fear, but of power and of love and of a sound mind." Overcoming fear begins with trusting in God's power and provision.

Parable: The Tightrope Walker

A famous tightrope walker announced he would cross a deep canyon on a thin wire, pushing a wheelbarrow. Crowds gathered, gasping as he skillfully moved across. At the other side, he asked, "Do you believe I can do it again?"

The crowd cheered, "Yes, we believe!" Then he asked, "Who will sit in the wheelbarrow while I cross?" The crowd fell silent.

Faith is not just believing that God can—it's trusting Him enough to take the risk. Like the tightrope walker, God calls us to trust Him fully, even when the path seems uncertain. True faith overcomes fear by placing our confidence in His abilities, not ours.

Faith That Overcomes

Throughout Scripture, God calls His people to step out in faith despite their fears. When God called Moses to lead Israel out of Egypt, Moses doubted his ability, saying, "Who am I that I should go to Pharaoh?" (Exodus 3:11). But God assured him, "I will certainly be with you" (Exodus 3:12 NKJV). Moses' faith grew as he relied on God's presence and strength.

Similarly, Peter stepped out of the boat and walked on water toward Jesus. When fear caused him to sink, Jesus reached out and said, "O you of little faith, why did you doubt?" (Matthew 14:31 NKJV). Both Moses and Peter remind us that overcoming fear requires stepping out in faith and keeping our eyes on God.

Walking in Courage

Overcoming fear doesn't mean never feeling afraid—it means choosing faith in the face of fear. Joshua 1:9 encourages, "Have I not commanded you? Be strong and of good courage; do not be afraid, nor be dismayed, for the Lord your God is with you wherever you go."

Faith grows as we act on God's promises, trusting that He will provide, protect, and guide us. Psalm 56:3 declares, "Whenever I am afraid, I will trust in You." Trusting God turns fear into courage and uncertainty into strength.

Reflection Questions

What fears are holding you back, and how can you surrender them to God?

_____

_____

_____

How can you take a step of faith, trusting God in the face of fear?

_____

_____

_____

In what ways can you remind yourself of God's promises when fear arises?

_____

_____

_____

Prayer Prompt

Lord, thank You for the assurance that You are with me in every situation. Teach me to trust in Your power and to face my fears with faith and courage. Help me to keep my eyes on You, knowing that Your presence casts out fear. Amen.

Day 14: Unpacking Bitterness

God's Call to Forgive

Forgiveness is one of the most powerful acts of love and faith. Jesus taught, "For if you forgive men their trespasses, your heavenly Father will also forgive you" (Matthew 6:14 NKJV). Forgiveness frees us from bitterness and aligns our hearts with God's grace.

Ephesians 4:32 encourages us, "And be kind to one another, tenderhearted, forgiving one another, even as God in Christ forgave you." As recipients of God's forgiveness, we are called to extend the same grace to others.

Parable: The Heavy Backpack

A traveler carried a heavy backpack filled with rocks, each one representing a grudge or resentment. As the journey grew longer, the weight became unbearable. Another traveler suggested, "Why not let go of the rocks? You don't need them."

Reluctantly, the traveler began discarding the rocks one by one. With each release, the burden grew lighter, and the journey became easier. By the time the traveler reached the destination, the once-overwhelming load was gone, replaced by a sense of freedom and peace.

Unforgiveness is like that heavy backpack—it weighs us down and hinders our journey. Letting go of bitterness allows us to walk in the freedom God desires for us.

Forgiveness Through Christ

Forgiving others can feel impossible, especially when the hurt runs deep. Yet Jesus modeled ultimate forgiveness on the cross, saying, "Father, forgive them, for they do not know what they do" (Luke 23:34 NKJV). His sacrifice empowers us to forgive, knowing that God's grace is sufficient for every situation.

Joseph's story is a powerful example of forgiveness. Despite being betrayed by his brothers, he chose to forgive, saying, "But as for you, you meant evil against me; but God meant it for good" (Genesis 50:20 NKJV). Forgiveness allowed Joseph to move forward and fulfill God's greater purpose.

The Freedom of Forgiveness

Forgiveness is not about excusing wrong behavior—it's about releasing ourselves from the grip of bitterness. Colossians 3:13 reminds us, "Forgive as the Lord forgave you." When we forgive, we experience healing and peace that only God can provide.

Forgiveness also opens the door for reconciliation and restoration. While not every relationship can be fully restored, forgiving others allows us to let go of the past and embrace the future with a clean heart.

Reflection Questions

What grudges or resentments are weighing you down, and how can you release them to God?

_____

_____

_____

How can remembering God's forgiveness toward you help you forgive others?

_____

_____

_____

In what ways can forgiveness bring freedom and healing to your life?

_____

_____

_____

Prayer Prompt

Lord, thank You for forgiving me and setting me free from my sins. Teach me to extend the same grace to others, even when it feels difficult. Help me to let go of bitterness and to walk in the freedom and peace that forgiveness brings. Amen.

Day 15: God's Guidance in Uncertainty

Trusting God's Direction

Life is filled with moments of uncertainty, but God promises to guide us. Proverbs 3:5-6 reminds us, "Trust in the Lord with all your heart, and lean not on your own understanding; in all your ways acknowledge Him, and He shall direct your paths." Trusting God means surrendering our plans and seeking His will above all else.

Psalm 32:8 assures us, "I will instruct you and teach you in the way you should go; I will guide you with My eye." God's guidance brings clarity and peace, even when the road ahead is unclear.

Parable: The Blindfolded Hiker

A group of hikers embarked on a journey with an unusual twist: one person in each pair was blindfolded and had to rely on their partner for guidance. The blindfolded hikers stumbled at first, hesitant to trust, but as they listened and followed their partners' directions, they navigated the trail with surprising ease.

At the end of the hike, one blindfolded participant said, "I couldn't see anything, but I trusted my partner's voice. That's what got me through."

In the same way, trusting God's guidance requires us to listen to His voice and step forward in faith, even when we can't see the full path. His perspective is greater than ours, and His direction is always reliable.

God's Word as Our Compass

The Bible is a powerful tool for discerning God's guidance. Psalm 119:105 says, "Your word is a lamp to my feet and a light to my path." By spending time in Scripture, we align our hearts with God's truth and receive wisdom for our decisions.

Prayer also plays a vital role in seeking God's guidance. James 1:5 encourages, "If any of you lacks wisdom, let him ask of God, who gives to all liberally and without reproach, and it will be given to him." Bringing our questions and uncertainties to God opens the door for His direction.

Walking in Faith

God often reveals His plan one step at a time, requiring us to walk in faith. Abraham exemplified this when God called him to leave his homeland without revealing the destination. Hebrews 11:8 says, "By faith Abraham obeyed when he was called to go out to the place which he would receive as an inheritance. And he went out, not knowing where he was going."

Faith doesn't eliminate uncertainty—it transforms it into an opportunity to trust God. As we take steps of obedience, His plan unfolds in ways that exceed our expectations.

Reflection Questions

In what areas of your life do you need to trust God's guidance more fully?

_____

_____

_____

How can you use Scripture and prayer to discern God's direction?

_____

_____

_____

What steps of faith can you take today to follow God's leading?

_____

_____

_____

Prayer Prompt

Lord, thank You for being my guide in every season of life. Teach me to trust in Your plans and to seek Your direction through prayer and Your Word. Help me to walk in faith, knowing that You see the full path ahead, even when I cannot. Amen.

Day 16: God's Presence in the Storm

Peace in the Midst of Chaos

Life's storms can leave us feeling overwhelmed and afraid, but God's presence brings peace and assurance. Isaiah 43:2 reminds us, "When you pass through the waters, I will be with you; and through the rivers, they shall not overflow you." God's promise to be with us is a constant source of comfort, even in the most challenging times.

Jesus said in John 16:33, "These things I have spoken to you, that in Me you may have peace. In the world you will have tribulation; but be of good cheer, I have overcome the world." His victory gives us hope and strength to endure life's storms.

Parable: The Unshakable Tree

In a vast forest, a fierce storm swept through, uprooting trees and leaving destruction in its path. Yet, one tree remained standing, its roots deep and unshaken. A traveler asked the tree, "How did you survive when so many others fell?"

The tree replied, "My roots are anchored deep into the rock beneath the soil. While the storm raged above, I was held steady by what is unseen."

Like the tree, we find stability in life's storms by anchoring ourselves in God's presence. Though the winds of adversity may howl, His strength holds us firm.

God's Power in the Storm

When Jesus calmed the storm, His disciples were amazed. Mark 4:39-40 recounts, "Then He arose and rebuked the wind, and said to the sea, 'Peace, be still!' And the wind ceased and there was a great calm. But He said to them, 'Why are you so fearful? How is it that you have no faith?'" This story reminds us that God has authority over every storm in our lives.

Faith in God's power allows us to focus on Him rather than our circumstances. Psalm 46:1-2 assures us, "God is our refuge and strength, a very present help in trouble. Therefore we will not fear, even though the earth be removed, and though the mountains be carried into the midst of the sea."

Walking Through the Storm

Storms are inevitable, but God uses them to strengthen our faith and draw us closer to Him. James 1:2-4 encourages, "My brethren, count it all joy when you fall into various trials, knowing that the testing of your faith produces patience. But let patience have its perfect work, that you may be perfect and complete, lacking nothing."

Walking through storms with God's presence transforms fear into faith and uncertainty into confidence. Trusting Him in the midst of chaos reveals His power and deepens our relationship with Him.

Reflection Questions

What storms are you facing, and how can you rely on God's presence to sustain you?

_____
_____
_____

How does focusing on God's power rather than your circumstances bring peace and confidence?

_____
_____
_____

In what ways has God used past storms to strengthen your faith and character?

_____
_____
_____

Prayer Prompt

Lord, thank You for being my refuge and strength in life's storms. Teach me to trust in Your power and to rest in the assurance of Your presence. Help me to walk through challenges with faith, knowing that You are always with me and that You have authority over every situation. Amen.

Day 17: God's Faithfulness in Every Season

God's Unchanging Nature

God's faithfulness is a cornerstone of our trust in Him. Lamentations 3:22-23 declares, "Through the Lord's mercies we are not consumed, because His compassions fail not. They are new every morning; great is Your faithfulness." In every season, God remains constant, providing grace and strength for each new day.

Hebrews 10:23 encourages us, "Let us hold fast the confession of our hope without wavering, for He who promised is faithful." No matter the challenges we face, God's faithfulness assures us that His promises are true and His presence is unwavering.

Parable: The Seasons of the Tree

A tree stood tall in the middle of a meadow, experiencing the full range of seasons. In the spring, its branches blossomed with vibrant flowers. In the summer, it bore abundant fruit. In autumn, its leaves turned golden and fell to the ground. During the harsh winter, it stood bare and seemingly lifeless.

Yet, through every season, the tree's roots remained deep and strong. No matter the external changes, its foundation sustained it, allowing it to thrive again when the seasons shifted.

In the same way, God's faithfulness is the root that sustains us through every season of life. Whether we are in a time of growth, harvest, or waiting, His presence anchors us and prepares us for what lies ahead.

Trusting God in Every Season

Life's seasons often bring uncertainty, but God's faithfulness gives us the courage to trust Him. Ecclesiastes 3:1 reminds us, "To everything there is a season, a time for every purpose under heaven." Trusting that God has a purpose for each season allows us to walk with faith and patience.

Joseph's life illustrates this truth. From the betrayal of his brothers to his rise as a leader in Egypt, Joseph experienced seasons of hardship and triumph. Through it all, he recognized God's hand at work, saying, "But as for you, you meant evil against me; but God meant it for good" (Genesis 50:20 NKJV).

God's Faithfulness in the Waiting

Waiting is one of the most challenging seasons, but it is also one of the most transformative. Isaiah 40:31 assures us, "But those who wait on the Lord shall renew their strength; they shall mount up with wings like eagles, they shall run and not be weary, they shall walk and not faint." Waiting on God refines our character and deepens our dependence on Him.

Abraham's journey of faith reminds us of the power of trusting God in the waiting. Though the promise of a son took years to fulfill, Abraham's faith was strengthened as he relied on God's unwavering faithfulness.

Reflection Questions

What season of life are you in, and how is God showing His faithfulness to you?

_____
_____
_____

How can you trust God more fully in seasons of waiting or uncertainty?

_____
_____
_____

In what ways has God's faithfulness sustained you in the past, and how does that encourage you now?

_____
_____
_____

Prayer Prompt

Lord, thank You for Your faithfulness that sustains me through every season of life. Help me to trust in Your plans and to rely on Your grace, even in times of waiting or hardship. Teach me to see Your hand at work in every circumstance, knowing that You are always with me. Amen.

Day 18: The Strength of Community

God's Design for Community

God created us to thrive in relationships with others. Ecclesiastes 4:9-10 reminds us, "Two are better than one, because they have a good reward for their labor. For if they fall, one will lift up his companion." Community strengthens, encourages, and supports us in our faith journey.

Hebrews 10:24-25 urges, "And let us consider one another in order to stir up love and good works, not forsaking the assembling of ourselves together, as is the manner of some, but exhorting one another." Being part of a community of believers helps us grow and stay connected to God's purpose.

Parable: The Ember in the Fire

A man sat by a fire on a cold night, watching the flames dance over the logs. He took one glowing ember and set it aside. Gradually, the ember dimmed and lost its warmth. The man then placed the ember back into the fire, and it reignited, glowing brightly once again.

Community is like the fire—when we isolate ourselves, we grow cold spiritually. But when we stay connected to others, we are reignited and strengthened by shared faith, encouragement, and love.

Unity in the Body of Christ

The church is described as the body of Christ, where each member plays a vital role. 1 Corinthians 12:12-14 explains, "For as the body is one and has many members, but all the members of that one body, being many, are one body, so also is Christ. For by one Spirit we were all baptized into one body." Each person's unique gifts contribute to the unity and mission of the church.

Jesus modeled the importance of community by surrounding Himself with disciples. He taught, prayed, and served alongside them, demonstrating how relationships can deepen faith and fulfill God's work.

The Power of Fellowship

Fellowship helps us grow spiritually and emotionally. Proverbs 27:17 says, "As iron sharpens iron, so a man sharpens the countenance of his friend." Through shared prayer, worship, and accountability, community fosters spiritual growth and keeps us rooted in God's truth.

Paul's letters often highlight the strength he drew from fellow believers. In 1 Thessalonians 5:11, he encourages, "Therefore comfort each other and edify one another, just as you also are doing." Supporting and uplifting one another reflects God's love and strengthens the entire community.

Reflection Questions

How has being part of a faith community strengthened your relationship with God?

_____

_____

_____

What steps can you take to deepen your connections with others in your community?

_____

_____

_____

How can you use your gifts to support and encourage those around you?

_____

_____

_____

Prayer Prompt

Lord, thank You for the gift of community and the strength it provides. Help me to build meaningful relationships that honor You and encourage others. Teach me to serve, love, and uplift those around me, so that we may grow together in faith and unity. Amen.

Day 19: The Joy of Obedience

Obedience as an Act of Worship

Obedience to God is an expression of love and trust. Jesus said, "If you love Me, keep My commandments" (John 14:15 NKJV). Obeying God's Word aligns our hearts with His will and deepens our relationship with Him.

Psalm 119:2 declares, "Blessed are those who keep His testimonies, who seek Him with the whole heart!" Obedience brings joy because it leads us into the fullness of God's blessings and purpose for our lives.

Parable: The Kite and the Wind

A kite soared high in the sky, marveling at its freedom. As the wind carried it higher, the kite thought, "If only I weren't tethered by this string, I could fly even farther." Determined to break free, the kite tugged and pulled until the string snapped.

For a brief moment, the kite floated freely. But without the string's guidance, it soon spiraled out of control and fell to the ground. It realized that the string it once resented had been the source of its ability to fly.

Like the kite, we often see obedience as a limitation, but it is the very thing that enables us to soar. God's commands are not restrictions but guidance that leads to freedom, joy, and fulfillment.

The Blessings of Obedience

Throughout Scripture, obedience is tied to blessings. Deuteronomy 28:1-2 promises, "Now it shall come to pass, if you diligently obey the voice of the Lord your God... that all these blessings shall come upon you and overtake you, because you obey the voice of the Lord your God."

Abraham's obedience to God's call is a powerful example. Despite not knowing where he was going, he followed God's direction, and his faithfulness led to the fulfillment of God's covenant promises (Genesis 12:1-4). His story reminds us that obedience opens the door to God's blessings and purposes.

Overcoming Fear of Obedience

Obedience often requires stepping out in faith and letting go of fear. When God called Jonah to preach to Nineveh, Jonah initially resisted, fearing the task. Yet, when he obeyed, God brought about an incredible revival (Jonah 3:1-10). Jonah's story teaches us that obedience, even when difficult, allows God to work powerfully through us.

Obedience is not about perfection—it's about surrender. Proverbs 3:5-6 encourages, "Trust in the Lord with all your heart, and lean not on your own understanding; in all your ways acknowledge Him, and He shall direct your paths." Trusting God's guidance gives us the courage to follow His commands.

Reflection Questions

How can you view obedience to God as an act of worship rather than a restriction?

_____

_____

_____

What areas of your life require greater trust and surrender to God's guidance?

_____

_____

_____

How has obedience to God brought joy or blessings into your life?

_____

_____

_____

Prayer Prompt

Lord, thank You for the gift of Your guidance and commands, which lead me into the fullness of Your blessings. Teach me to trust in Your wisdom and to obey with joy and faith. Help me to surrender my fears and follow You wholeheartedly, knowing that Your ways are always best. Amen.

Day 20: God's Faithfulness in Trials

Trusting God in Difficult Times

Trials are an inevitable part of life, but God's faithfulness never wavers. James 1:2-3 encourages us, "My brethren, count it all joy when you fall into various trials, knowing that the testing of your faith produces patience." Trusting God in difficult times deepens our faith and draws us closer to Him.

Isaiah 43:2 reminds us, "When you pass through the waters, I will be with you; and through the rivers, they shall not overflow you." God's presence is constant, offering strength and comfort in every challenge.

Parable: The Blacksmith's Forge

A blacksmith worked tirelessly, heating and hammering metal into a perfect shape. A curious apprentice asked, "Why do you put the metal through such intense heat and pressure?"

The blacksmith replied, "To remove impurities and strengthen it. Without the fire, it would remain weak and unusable. The process is tough, but it brings out the metal's true potential."

Like the blacksmith, God uses trials to refine and strengthen us. Though the process may feel intense, it prepares us for the purposes He has planned for our lives.

God's Faithfulness in Refinement

Trials often reveal God's faithfulness in unexpected ways. Job's story exemplifies this truth. Despite losing everything, Job held onto his faith, declaring, "But He knows the way that I take; when He has tested me, I shall come forth as gold" (Job 23:10 NKJV). God restored Job's fortunes, demonstrating His compassion and purpose in trials.

Paul also experienced God's faithfulness in trials. He wrote in 2 Corinthians 12:9, "My grace is sufficient for you, for My strength is made perfect in weakness." God's grace sustains us, turning our weaknesses into opportunities for His power to shine.

Finding Purpose in Trials

God often uses trials to prepare us for greater things. Joseph's journey from slavery to leadership in Egypt is a powerful reminder of this truth. What seemed like setbacks were actually steps in God's plan. Joseph later declared, "You meant evil against me; but God meant it for good" (Genesis 50:20 NKJV).

Our trials are never wasted in God's hands. Romans 8:28 assures us, "And we know that all things work together for good to those who love God, to those who are the called according to His purpose." Trusting this promise gives us hope and strength to endure.

Reflection Questions

How have trials in your life revealed God's faithfulness and purpose?

___

In what ways can you trust God more deeply during difficult times?

___

How can you encourage others who are going through trials by sharing your testimony?

___

Prayer Prompt

Lord, thank You for Your faithfulness in every season of life, especially during trials. Teach me to trust in Your plan and to see challenges as opportunities for growth and refinement. Help me to rest in Your grace and to encourage others with the hope You provide. Amen.

Day 21: Walking in Faith

Faith as Our Foundation

Faith is the cornerstone of our relationship with God. Hebrews 11:1 defines it as "the substance of things hoped for, the evidence of things not seen." Walking in faith requires trusting God even when we don't have all the answers or see the full picture.

2 Corinthians 5:7 encourages us, "For we walk by faith, not by sight." Faith moves us beyond what we can see and into the realm of God's possibilities.

Parable: The Bridge in the Fog

A traveler approached a deep canyon shrouded in dense fog. A narrow bridge stretched across, but the traveler hesitated, unable to see the other side. A local assured him, "The bridge is sturdy. Many have crossed safely before you."

With trembling steps, the traveler began to walk. Though the other side remained hidden, each step revealed more of the bridge until he reached solid ground. When he looked back, he marveled at how the unseen had become clear through his faith.

Walking in faith is like crossing that bridge. We may not see the entire path, but trusting God allows us to move forward one step at a time, knowing He has already prepared the way.

Faith in Action

Faith is not passive—it requires action. James 2:17 reminds us, "Thus also faith by itself, if it does not have works, is dead." Acting on our faith demonstrates our trust in God's promises and His power to fulfill them.

Abraham exemplified this when God asked him to leave his homeland and go to an unknown land. Hebrews 11:8 says, "By faith Abraham obeyed when he was called to go out to the place which he would receive as an inheritance." His obedience, despite the uncertainty, was a testament to his faith.

Faith in God's Promises

God's promises are the foundation of our faith. Romans 4:20-21 highlights Abraham's unwavering trust: "He did not waver at the promise of God through unbelief, but was strengthened in faith, giving glory to God, and being fully convinced that what He had promised He was also able to perform."

Faith grows as we stand on God's Word and trust Him to fulfill what He has spoken. Hebrews 11 is filled with examples of those who walked in faith, each one a reminder of God's faithfulness to those who trust Him.

Reflection Questions

What steps of faith is God calling you to take in your life right now?

_____

_____

_____

How can you trust God's promises even when the path ahead seems unclear?

_____

_____

_____

In what ways has walking in faith strengthened your relationship with God?

_____

_____

_____

Prayer Prompt

Lord, thank You for being the foundation of my faith. Teach me to trust in Your promises and to take bold steps of obedience, even when the path is uncertain. Help me to walk by faith and not by sight, knowing that You are always leading me. Amen.

Day 22: God's Comfort in Times of Grief

The Promise of Comfort

Grief is a natural part of life, but God promises to be our source of comfort in times of sorrow. Matthew 5:4 assures us, "Blessed are those who mourn, for they shall be comforted." God's presence brings healing and peace to the brokenhearted.

Psalm 34:18 reminds us, "The Lord is near to those who have a broken heart, and saves such as have a contrite spirit." His nearness provides strength and hope, even in the midst of loss.

Parable: The Broken Vase

A woman treasured a beautiful porcelain vase that had been in her family for generations. One day, the vase fell and shattered into countless pieces. Heartbroken, she collected the fragments and considered discarding them. Instead, she began the painstaking process of repairing it.

Using gold lacquer to fill the cracks, she transformed the broken vase into something even more beautiful. The golden lines told a story of restoration and resilience.

Like the vase, our grief can feel shattering, but God's comfort fills the cracks with His healing presence, creating something even more beautiful in the process. He redeems our pain and brings purpose to our brokenness.

God's Presence in Grief

God's presence is our refuge during times of sorrow. Psalm 23:4 declares, "Yea, though I walk through the valley of the shadow of death, I will fear no evil; for You are with me; Your rod and Your staff, they comfort me." Walking through grief with God transforms despair into hope.

Jesus Himself experienced grief when He wept over Lazarus's death (John 11:35). His response shows us that God understands our pain and is deeply moved by our struggles. He meets us in our sorrow with compassion and care.

Finding Hope in God's Promises

Grief often causes us to question and seek meaning, but God's promises bring hope. Revelation 21:4 offers this assurance: "And God will wipe away every tear from their eyes; there shall be no more death, nor sorrow, nor crying. There shall be no more pain, for the former things have passed away."

Paul also encourages us with the hope of resurrection: "For if we believe that Jesus died and rose again, even so God will bring with Him those who sleep in Jesus" (1 Thessalonians 4:14 NKJV). Trusting in God's eternal plan gives us peace, even in the face of loss.

Reflection Questions

How has God's presence comforted you during times of grief or loss?

_____

_____

_____

In what ways can you rely on God's promises to find hope in difficult times?

_____
_____
_____

How can you share God's comfort with others who are grieving?

_____
_____
_____

Prayer Prompt

Lord, thank You for being my comforter in times of sorrow. Help me to lean on Your presence and to trust in Your promises of healing and hope. Teach me to find peace in Your love and to share Your comfort with those who are grieving. Amen.

Day 23: God's Joy in Every Circumstance

Joy Beyond Circumstances

True joy comes from God and is not dependent on our external situations. Nehemiah 8:10 declares, "Do not sorrow, for the joy of the Lord is your strength." God's joy sustains us, giving us strength and peace in every season of life.

Paul encourages us in Philippians 4:4, "Rejoice in the Lord always. Again I will say, rejoice!" Choosing joy, even in difficult times, reflects our trust in God's sovereignty and faithfulness.

Parable: The Singing Prisoner

A man was unjustly imprisoned in a dark, damp cell. Instead of succumbing to despair, he began to sing praises to God. Fellow prisoners were astounded, asking, "How can you rejoice in a place like this?"

He replied, "My joy doesn't come from where I am—it comes from who God is. His goodness remains, no matter my circumstances."

Over time, his joy became contagious, bringing hope to others in the prison. Like the singing prisoner, when we focus on God's unchanging character rather than our circumstances, we experience a joy that transcends every situation.

Joy Rooted in God's Presence

Joy is a fruit of the Spirit that grows when we remain connected to God. Psalm 16:11 reminds us, "You will show me the path of life; in Your presence is fullness of joy; at Your right hand are pleasures forevermore."

Spending time in God's presence through prayer, worship, and His Word fills us with lasting joy.

Jesus promised this joy to His disciples: "These things I have spoken to you, that My joy may remain in you, and that your joy may be full" (John 15:11 NKJV). His joy strengthens us and equips us to face life's challenges with confidence.

Choosing Joy in Difficult Times

Joy is not the absence of difficulty but the presence of God in the midst of it. James 1:2-3 encourages, "My brethren, count it all joy when you fall into various trials, knowing that the testing of your faith produces patience." Trials can deepen our dependence on God and reveal His faithfulness.

Paul and Silas modeled this truth in Acts 16:25. Imprisoned and beaten, they prayed and sang hymns to God, choosing joy over despair. Their faith not only brought personal peace but also led to a miraculous prison break and the salvation of the jailer and his family.

Reflection Questions

How can you choose joy in the midst of your current circumstances?

_____

_____

_____

In what ways has God's presence brought you strength and joy during challenging times?

_____

_____

_____

How can you cultivate joy daily by focusing on God's character and promises?

_____

_____

_____

Prayer Prompt

Lord, thank You for the joy that comes from knowing You. Teach me to choose joy in every circumstance and to trust in Your goodness and faithfulness. Help me to reflect Your joy to others, bringing hope and encouragement wherever I go. Amen.

Day 24: God's Protection in Uncertainty

The Promise of Protection

God promises to be our refuge and protector in times of trouble. Psalm 91:1-2 assures us, "He who dwells in the secret place of the Most High shall abide under the shadow of the Almighty. I will say of the Lord, 'He is my refuge and my fortress; my God, in Him I will trust.'" Trusting in God's protection gives us peace, even in the face of uncertainty.

Proverbs 18:10 reminds us, "The name of the Lord is a strong tower; the righteous run to it and are safe." His presence is a place of safety and security for those who seek Him.

Parable: The Sparrow in the Storm

During a violent storm, a farmer noticed a small sparrow perched calmly under the shelter of his barn's eaves. While other animals scrambled for safety, the sparrow remained still, trusting its protected spot. The farmer marveled at how the bird's peace came from knowing it was under strong, unshakable shelter.

Like the sparrow, we find peace in life's storms when we rest in God's protection. He is our shelter, steadfast and unmovable, no matter how fierce the storm around us becomes.

God's Faithfulness as Our Protector

The Bible is filled with examples of God's protection over His people. When the Israelites faced the Red Sea with Pharaoh's army behind them, God parted the waters, providing a miraculous way of escape (Exodus

14:21-22). His protection turned an impossible situation into a testament of His power and faithfulness.

Daniel experienced God's protection in the lions' den. Though he faced what seemed like certain death, God sent His angel to shut the mouths of the lions (Daniel 6:22). These stories remind us that no situation is beyond God's ability to protect and deliver.

Trusting God's Plan

Sometimes, God's protection doesn't look the way we expect. Paul faced numerous trials, including shipwrecks and imprisonments, yet he trusted God's plan. In Acts 27, God's guidance and protection preserved Paul and the ship's crew during a storm. Paul's faith in God's sovereignty helped him endure and fulfill his mission.

Isaiah 41:10 encourages us, "Fear not, for I am with you; be not dismayed, for I am your God. I will strengthen you, yes, I will help you, I will uphold you with My righteous right hand." Trusting God's plan, even in uncertainty, allows us to walk in confidence and peace.

Reflection Questions

In what areas of your life do you need to trust more in God's protection?

_____

_____

_____

How has God's faithfulness been a source of safety and peace during uncertain times?

_____

_____

_____

What steps can you take to seek God's shelter through prayer and trust in His promises?

_____

_____

_____

Prayer Prompt

Lord, thank You for being my refuge and protector in every season. Teach me to trust in Your power and faithfulness, even when life feels uncertain. Help me to rest in Your promises and to walk confidently, knowing that You are my shield and fortress. Amen.

Day 25: The Strength of Patience

Patience as a Virtue

Patience is a fruit of the Spirit that helps us endure trials and trust in God's timing. James 5:7-8 encourages, "Therefore be patient, brethren, until the coming of the Lord. See how the farmer waits for the precious fruit of the earth, waiting patiently for it until it receives the early and latter rain. You also be patient." Patience is not passive but an active trust in God's work.

Romans 12:12 reminds us to be "rejoicing in hope, patient in tribulation, continuing steadfastly in prayer." Patience strengthens our faith and keeps us aligned with God's plans.

Parable: The Sculptor's Vision

A sculptor worked tirelessly on a large block of marble. Day after day, he chipped away at the stone, his progress slow and painstaking. Onlookers grew impatient, asking, "Why is it taking so long? Can't you hurry?"

The sculptor replied, "It takes time to reveal the masterpiece within. Every stroke matters, and rushing would ruin the beauty I see."

Much like the sculptor, God is working on us, shaping and refining us in His perfect time. Patience allows us to trust the process, knowing that God's masterpiece is worth the wait.

Patience in God's Plan

God often uses seasons of waiting to grow our faith and character. Abraham waited 25 years for the fulfillment of God's promise of a son, yet he remained faithful. Romans 4:20-21 says, "He did not waver at the promise of God through unbelief, but was strengthened in faith, giving glory to God."

Joseph's journey is another example. From being sold into slavery to rising as a leader in Egypt, Joseph endured years of waiting and hardship. His patience and trust in God's plan led to the fulfillment of a greater purpose (Genesis 50:20).

Finding Strength in the Wait

Waiting can be challenging, but it is also transformative. Isaiah 40:31 assures us, "But those who wait on the Lord shall renew their strength; they shall mount up with wings like eagles, they shall run and not be weary, they shall walk and not faint." Patience allows us to rely on God's strength rather than our own.

Paul encourages us to remain steadfast in the waiting: "And let us not grow weary while doing good, for in due season we shall reap if we do not lose heart" (Galatians 6:9). Trusting in God's timing gives us hope and perseverance.

Reflection Questions

In what areas of your life do you need to practice more patience and trust in God's timing?

_____

_____

_____

How has waiting on God in the past strengthened your faith and character?

_____

_____

_____

What steps can you take to cultivate patience in your daily life?

_____

_____

_____

Prayer Prompt

Lord, thank You for the strength that comes from patience and trust in Your timing. Teach me to wait on You with faith and perseverance, knowing that You are working for my good. Help me to see the purpose in the process and to rely on Your wisdom in every season. Amen.

Day 26: God's Provision in Every Need

The Promise of Provision

God promises to supply all our needs according to His riches in glory. Philippians 4:19 assures us, "And my God shall supply all your need according to His riches in glory by Christ Jesus." Trusting in God's provision frees us from worry and strengthens our faith.

Jesus reminds us in Matthew 6:26, "Look at the birds of the air, for they neither sow nor reap nor gather into barns; yet your heavenly Father feeds them. Are you not of more value than they?" God's care for creation reflects His abundant love and provision for us.

Parable: The Empty Pantry

A widow and her young son faced a harsh winter with little food left in their pantry. One evening, as she prayed for provision, there was a knock at the door. A neighbor arrived with bags of groceries, saying, "I felt led to bring this to you today."

Moved to tears, the widow realized that God had used her neighbor to answer her prayer. What seemed like a hopeless situation became a testimony of God's faithfulness to provide, often in unexpected ways.

Like the widow, trusting God in moments of scarcity allows Him to demonstrate His ability to meet our needs beyond what we can imagine.

God's Provision in Scripture

The Bible is filled with examples of God's miraculous provision. When Elijah stayed with a widow during a famine, her flour and oil never ran out, despite having only a small amount to begin with (1 Kings 17:14-16). God multiplied her resources because of her faith and obedience.

Jesus fed a crowd of over 5,000 people with just five loaves of bread and two fish (Matthew 14:17-21). His provision not only met the immediate need but left an abundance of leftovers, demonstrating His ability to exceed our expectations.

Trusting God in Uncertainty

Relying on God's provision requires faith, especially in uncertain times. Proverbs 3:5-6 encourages, "Trust in the Lord with all your heart, and lean not on your own understanding; in all your ways acknowledge Him, and He shall direct your paths." God's provision often comes in ways we don't expect but always at the right time.

The Israelites experienced this in the wilderness. Despite their doubts, God provided manna from heaven daily to sustain them (Exodus 16:4-5). His faithfulness reminds us that He knows our needs and is always working on our behalf.

Reflection Questions

How has God provided for you in times of need, even in unexpected ways?

_____

_____

_____

In what areas of your life do you need to trust God more fully for His provision?

_____

_____

_____

How can you use your own blessings to help meet the needs of others?

_____

_____

_____

Prayer Prompt

Lord, thank You for being my provider in every season of life. Help me to trust in Your faithfulness and to rely on Your promises. Teach me to recognize Your provision, even in unexpected ways, and to share my blessings with those in need. Amen.

Day 27: God's Peace in Chaos

The Gift of Peace

God's peace is a gift that surpasses all understanding. Jesus promised, "Peace I leave with you, My peace I give to you; not as the world gives do I give to you. Let not your heart be troubled, neither let it be afraid" (John 14:27 NKJV). His peace is not dependent on circumstances but flows from His presence in our lives.

Philippians 4:6-7 encourages, "Be anxious for nothing, but in everything by prayer and supplication, with thanksgiving, let your requests be made known to God; and the peace of God, which surpasses all understanding, will guard your hearts and minds through Christ Jesus."

Parable: The Calm Painter

A king announced a contest for artists to create a painting that captured the essence of peace. Many submissions depicted tranquil landscapes and serene waters. However, the winning painting showed a raging storm with lightning and crashing waves. In the center of the storm was a small bird, calmly perched in its nest, completely undisturbed.

The king explained, "True peace is not the absence of chaos but the presence of calm in its midst."

In the same way, God's peace doesn't eliminate life's storms—it sustains us through them. His presence enables us to remain calm and confident, no matter the chaos around us.

Peace in God's Presence

Peace is found in God's presence, not in the absence of trouble. Psalm 46:1-2 reminds us, "God is our refuge and strength, a very present help in trouble. Therefore we will not fear, even though the earth be removed, and though the mountains be carried into the midst of the sea." Trusting in God's presence brings stability in uncertain times.

When Jesus calmed the storm on the Sea of Galilee, He asked His disciples, "Why are you so fearful? How is it that you have no faith?" (Mark 4:40 NKJV). This story teaches us to focus on Jesus rather than the storm, knowing that He has authority over every situation.

Living in Peace

Living in God's peace requires us to surrender our fears and trust in His sovereignty. Isaiah 26:3 declares, "You will keep him in perfect peace, whose mind is stayed on You, because he trusts in You." By fixing our thoughts on God, we align our hearts with His truth and experience lasting peace.

Paul encourages us in Colossians 3:15, "And let the peace of God rule in your hearts." Peace is a choice that grows through prayer, gratitude, and reliance on God's promises.

Reflection Questions

What areas of your life feel chaotic, and how can you invite God's peace into those situations?

_____

_____

_____

How has God's peace sustained you during past challenges or storms?

_____

_____

_____

What practices can help you focus on God's presence and experience His peace daily?

_____

_____

_____

Prayer Prompt

Lord, thank You for the gift of Your peace that calms my heart in every storm. Teach me to trust in Your presence and to surrender my fears to You. Help me to live with a calm and confident spirit, knowing that You are in control of every situation. Amen.

Day 28: God's Wisdom for Life's Decisions

The Gift of God's Wisdom

God offers His wisdom to guide us through life's decisions. James 1:5 encourages, "If any of you lacks wisdom, let him ask of God, who gives to all liberally and without reproach, and it will be given to him." Seeking God's wisdom equips us to make choices that align with His will and purpose.

Proverbs 3:5-6 reminds us, "Trust in the Lord with all your heart, and lean not on your own understanding; in all your ways acknowledge Him, and He shall direct your paths." Trusting God's guidance brings clarity and peace to even the most difficult decisions.

Parable: The Two Builders

Two men set out to build homes. One chose a plot of sand, eager to complete his house quickly. The other selected a solid rock foundation, taking time to prepare the site. When storms came, the house on the sand collapsed, while the house on the rock stood firm.

The builder on the rock explained, "I trusted the process, even when it took longer. A strong foundation was worth the wait."

Similarly, seeking God's wisdom ensures that our decisions are built on a solid foundation, enabling us to withstand life's storms. Rushing into choices without God's guidance often leads to instability, while trusting His direction brings lasting peace.

God's Word as Our Guide

God's Word is a source of wisdom for every aspect of life. Psalm 119:105 says, "Your word is a lamp to my feet and a light to my path." By meditating on Scripture, we gain insight into God's principles and His plans for our lives.

The Bible is filled with examples of those who sought God's wisdom. King Solomon prayed for wisdom to lead Israel, and God granted his request, making him renowned for his discernment (1 Kings 3:9-12). Solomon's story reminds us that wisdom begins with humility and a desire to honor God.

Trusting God in Uncertainty

Making decisions often involves uncertainty, but God's wisdom provides confidence. Proverbs 16:9 reminds us, "A man's heart plans his way, but the Lord directs his steps." Trusting God's direction allows us to move forward in faith, even when the path ahead isn't clear.

Jesus modeled reliance on God's wisdom in His earthly ministry, often withdrawing to pray before making significant decisions (Luke 6:12-13). His example teaches us the importance of seeking God's guidance in every step.

Reflection Questions

What decisions in your life require God's wisdom and guidance right now?

_____

_____

_____

How can you use Scripture and prayer to align your choices with God's will?

_____

_____

_____

In what ways has trusting God's wisdom led to peace and clarity in your life?

_____

_____

_____

Prayer Prompt

Lord, thank You for the gift of Your wisdom that guides me in every decision. Teach me to seek Your direction through prayer and Your Word. Help me to trust Your timing and to make choices that honor You, knowing that You are leading me on the right path. Amen.

Day 29: The Courage to Trust God

Courage Through Faith

Trusting God often requires courage, especially when the path ahead is uncertain. Joshua 1:9 encourages, "Have I not commanded you? Be strong and of good courage; do not be afraid, nor be dismayed, for the Lord your God is with you wherever you go." Courage comes from knowing that God is always with us.

Psalm 56:3 reminds us, "Whenever I am afraid, I will trust in You." Choosing to trust God in the face of fear deepens our faith and strengthens our resolve.

Parable: The Cliff Diver

A young man stood at the edge of a towering cliff, hesitating to jump into the crystal-clear waters below. His friends cheered him on, saying, "The water is deep, and we've jumped safely before. You just have to trust."

Gathering his courage, he leapt off the edge, feeling the rush of freedom as he plunged into the water. When he surfaced, he exclaimed, "The hardest part was letting go of my fear."

Trusting God often feels like standing at the edge of a cliff. Letting go of fear and taking the leap requires courage, but it leads to the joy and freedom that come from trusting His promises.

Biblical Examples of Courage

The Bible is filled with stories of individuals who demonstrated courage by trusting God. David faced Goliath with confidence, declaring, "The Lord, who delivered me from the paw of the lion and from the paw of the bear, He will deliver me from the hand of this Philistine" (1 Samuel 17:37 NKJV). His faith in God's power gave him the courage to face a giant.

Esther risked her life to approach the king and save her people, saying, "If I perish, I perish!" (Esther 4:16 NKJV). Her courage came from trusting in God's purpose for her life, even in the face of great danger.

Courage in Everyday Life

Trusting God with our everyday decisions also requires courage. Proverbs 3:5-6 reminds us, "Trust in the Lord with all your heart, and lean not on your own understanding; in all your ways acknowledge Him, and He shall direct your paths." Courage comes from releasing control and allowing God to guide us.

Jesus set the ultimate example of courage by trusting God's plan, even as He faced the cross. In the Garden of Gethsemane, He prayed, "Not My will, but Yours, be done" (Luke 22:42 NKJV). His obedience reminds us that courage is not the absence of fear but the decision to trust God in spite of it.

Reflection Questions

What areas of your life require courage to trust God more fully?

_____

_____

_____

How can you draw inspiration from biblical examples of courage?

_____

_____

_____

In what ways has trusting God in difficult situations strengthened your faith?

_____

_____

_____

Prayer Prompt

Lord, thank You for being my source of courage in every situation. Teach me to trust in Your promises and to let go of fear, knowing that You are always with me. Help me to walk in faith and to face life's challenges with confidence in Your plan. Amen.

Day 30: God's Strength in Our Weakness

God's Power Made Perfect

Our weaknesses are not barriers to God—they are opportunities for His strength to shine. 2 Corinthians 12:9 reminds us, "And He said to me, 'My grace is sufficient for you, for My strength is made perfect in weakness.'" Embracing our limitations allows God's power to work through us.

Isaiah 40:29 declares, "He gives power to the weak, and to those who have no might He increases strength." Trusting in God's strength transforms our perspective on challenges and equips us to face them with confidence.

Parable: The Broken Bucket

A servant carried water each day using two buckets. One bucket was flawless, while the other had a crack and leaked water along the path. The cracked bucket felt ashamed, saying, "I'm not good enough to carry water like the other bucket."

The servant replied, "But look at the flowers along your side of the path. Your leaks have watered them, bringing beauty to this journey."

Like the cracked bucket, our weaknesses can feel like flaws, but God uses them to create beauty and purpose. His strength fills the gaps, turning our limitations into blessings.

God's Strength in Scripture

The Bible is filled with stories of God using weak individuals to accomplish great things. Moses doubted his ability to lead Israel out of Egypt, saying, "O my Lord, I am not eloquent" (Exodus 4:10 NKJV). Yet God chose him to deliver His people, reminding Moses, "I will be with your mouth and teach you what you shall say" (Exodus 4:12 NKJV).

Gideon, too, felt inadequate, calling himself the least in his family. But God used him to lead Israel to victory, saying, "Surely I will be with you, and you shall defeat the Midianites as one man" (Judges 6:16 NKJV). These stories remind us that God's strength is greater than our weaknesses.

Living in God's Strength

Acknowledging our weaknesses allows us to depend on God's power. Philippians 4:13 declares, "I can do all things through Christ who strengthens me." When we rely on Him, we find strength to face challenges and fulfill His purpose.

Paul's words in 2 Corinthians 4:7 illustrate this truth: "But we have this treasure in earthen vessels, that the excellence of the power may be of God and not of us." Our lives become vessels for God's strength and glory when we surrender our limitations to Him.

Reflection Questions

What weaknesses in your life can you surrender to God for His strength to shine through?

_____

_____

_____

How can you shift your perspective to see your limitations as opportunities for God's power?

_____

_____

_____

In what ways has God's strength been evident in your past challenges?

_____

_____

_____

Prayer Prompt

Lord, thank You for Your strength that is made perfect in my weakness. Teach me to trust in Your power and to surrender my limitations to You. Help me to see my challenges as opportunities for Your glory to be revealed in my life. Amen.

Day 31: Soaring After the Storm

God's Power Made Perfect

Our weaknesses are not barriers to God—they are opportunities for His strength to shine. 2 Corinthians 12:9 reminds us, "And He said to me, 'My grace is sufficient for you, for My strength is made perfect in weakness.'" Embracing our limitations allows God's power to work through us.

Isaiah 40:29 declares, "He gives power to the weak, and to those who have no might He increases strength." Trusting in God's strength transforms our perspective on challenges and equips us to face them with confidence.

Parable: The Weary Eagle

An eagle was soaring high above the mountains when a storm suddenly struck. Buffeted by strong winds, the eagle grew weary and began to falter. Spotting a towering tree, the eagle perched on a sturdy branch, resting as the storm raged around it.

When the storm subsided, the eagle took flight again, its strength renewed. It soared even higher than before, using the storm's winds to rise to greater heights.

Like the eagle, our moments of weakness are opportunities to rest in God's strength. He provides the shelter and renewal we need to rise above life's challenges, carrying us higher than we could ever go on our own.

God's Strength in Scripture

The Bible is filled with stories of God using weak individuals to accomplish great things. Moses doubted his ability to lead Israel out of Egypt, saying, "O my Lord, I am not eloquent" (Exodus 4:10 NKJV). Yet God chose him to deliver His people, reminding Moses, "I will be with your mouth and teach you what you shall say" (Exodus 4:12 NKJV).

Gideon, too, felt inadequate, calling himself the least in his family. But God used him to lead Israel to victory, saying, "Surely I will be with you, and you shall defeat the Midianites as one man" (Judges 6:16 NKJV). These stories remind us that God's strength is greater than our weaknesses.

Living in God's Strength

Acknowledging our weaknesses allows us to depend on God's power. Philippians 4:13 declares, "I can do all things through Christ who strengthens me." When we rely on Him, we find strength to face challenges and fulfill His purpose.

Paul's words in 2 Corinthians 4:7 illustrate this truth: "But we have this treasure in earthen vessels, that the excellence of the power may be of God and not of us." Our lives become vessels for God's strength and glory when we surrender our limitations to Him.

Reflection Questions

What weaknesses in your life can you surrender to God for His strength to shine through?

_____
_____
_____

How can you shift your perspective to see your limitations as opportunities for God's power?

_____
_____
_____

In what ways has God's strength been evident in your past challenges?

_____
_____
_____

Prayer Prompt

Lord, thank You for Your strength that is made perfect in my weakness. Teach me to trust in Your power and to surrender my limitations to You. Help me to see my challenges as opportunities for Your glory to be revealed in my life. Amen.

Day 32: The Light of God's Word

God's Word as Our Guide

The Bible is a lamp that illuminates our path, guiding us through life's uncertainties. Psalm 119:105 declares, "Your word is a lamp to my feet and a light to my path." God's Word provides clarity, wisdom, and direction for every decision we face.

Jesus emphasized the power of Scripture in Matthew 4:4: "Man shall not live by bread alone, but by every word that proceeds from the mouth of God." His Word nourishes our souls and equips us for every situation.

Parable: The Lost Traveler

A traveler set out on a journey through dense woods but lost his way as darkness fell. Struggling to find the path, he spotted a faint light in the distance. As he moved closer, he discovered a lantern left by another traveler, lighting the way forward. With the lantern's guidance, he safely navigated his way out of the forest.

God's Word is like that lantern. Even in the darkest moments of life, it provides the light we need to take the next step. Trusting in His Word allows us to walk confidently, knowing that He is leading us.

God's Word as a Source of Wisdom

The Bible offers wisdom for every aspect of life. Proverbs 2:6 says, "For the Lord gives wisdom; from His mouth come knowledge and understanding." Meditating on Scripture helps us discern God's will and make choices that honor Him.

When Joshua took over leadership of Israel, God instructed him, "This Book of the Law shall not depart from your mouth, but you shall meditate in it day and night, that you may observe to do according to all that is written in it. For then you will make your way prosperous, and then you will have good success" (Joshua 1:8 NKJV). Obedience to God's Word brings blessings and clarity.

Living in the Light

Living in the light of God's Word means allowing it to shape our thoughts, actions, and decisions. Psalm 1:2-3 describes the blessings of delighting in God's Word: "But his delight is in the law of the Lord, and in His law he meditates day and night. He shall be like a tree planted by the rivers of water, that brings forth its fruit in its season."

By aligning our lives with Scripture, we become rooted in God's truth, flourishing in every season. His Word transforms us, equipping us to reflect His light to the world.

Reflection Questions

How has God's Word guided you through difficult decisions or uncertain times?

_____

_____

_____

What practices can you adopt to deepen your understanding and application of Scripture?

_____
_____
_____

In what ways can you share the light of God's Word with others?

_____
_____
_____

Prayer Prompt

Lord, thank You for the light of Your Word that guides me through life's challenges. Teach me to meditate on Your truth and to apply it to my daily decisions. Help me to trust in Your promises and to share the hope of Your Word with those around me. Amen.

Day 33: God's Power in Prayer

The Power of Communicating with God

Prayer is a powerful way to connect with God and align our hearts with His will. James 5:16 declares, "The effective, fervent prayer of a righteous man avails much." Through prayer, we experience God's presence, guidance, and power in our lives.

Philippians 4:6-7 encourages us, "Be anxious for nothing, but in everything by prayer and supplication, with thanksgiving, let your requests be made known to God; and the peace of God, which surpasses all understanding, will guard your hearts and minds through Christ Jesus." Prayer not only changes circumstances but also transforms our hearts.

Parable: The Parched Field

A farmer's field lay dry and barren during a long drought. Despite the conditions, the farmer went out every day to prepare the soil, plant seeds, and pray for rain. Neighbors mocked his efforts, saying, "Why bother? Nothing will grow in this dry land."

One morning, dark clouds gathered, and rain poured down, soaking the prepared soil. The farmer's persistence and faith turned the barren field into a flourishing harvest.

Like the farmer, persistent prayer prepares the soil of our lives for God's blessings. Even when answers seem delayed, trusting in God's timing allows His power to work in ways we cannot yet see.

Biblical Examples of Prayer

The Bible is filled with examples of God's power revealed through prayer. Elijah prayed for rain after a three-year drought, and God answered, sending a downpour that restored the land (1 Kings 18:42-45). His faith and persistence demonstrate the importance of trusting God's timing.

Jesus modeled a life of prayer, often withdrawing to pray before major decisions and miracles. In Luke 6:12, He spent the night in prayer before selecting His disciples. His example reminds us that prayer is essential for seeking God's wisdom and strength.

The Transforming Power of Prayer

Prayer not only changes circumstances but also aligns us with God's purposes. Romans 12:12 encourages us, "Rejoicing in hope, patient in tribulation, continuing steadfastly in prayer." Persistent prayer strengthens our faith and keeps us focused on God's promises.

Through prayer, we surrender our fears, desires, and burdens to God, trusting Him to work for our good. Matthew 7:7 reminds us, "Ask, and it will be given to you; seek, and you will find; knock, and it will be opened to you." God invites us to approach Him with boldness and faith.

Reflection Questions

How has persistent prayer impacted your life or brought about change in difficult circumstances?

_____

_____

_____

What areas of your life do you need to surrender to God in prayer?

_____

_____

_____

How can you deepen your relationship with God through consistent and fervent prayer?

_____

_____

_____

Prayer Prompt

Lord, thank You for the gift of prayer that allows me to connect with You and seek Your guidance. Teach me to pray with persistence and faith, trusting in Your power and timing. Help me to surrender my worries to You and to walk in the peace that only You can provide. Amen.

Day 34: Strength of Perseverance

Endurance Through Faith

Perseverance is essential for fulfilling God's purposes in our lives. Galatians 6:9 encourages, "And let us not grow weary while doing good, for in due season we shall reap if we do not lose heart." God calls us to endure challenges with faith, trusting that our efforts will bear fruit.

James 1:12 reminds us, "Blessed is the man who endures temptation; for when he has been approved, he will receive the crown of life which the Lord has promised to those who love Him." Perseverance strengthens our faith and aligns us with God's eternal promises.

Parable: The Climbing Goat

A young mountain goat was determined to reach the highest peak, where lush grass awaited. The climb was steep and filled with obstacles, and the goat often stumbled. Older goats told him, "It's too hard; turn back."

But the young goat pressed on, step by step. When he finally reached the top, he found not only the green pastures but also a breathtaking view. Looking back at the path, he realized that every challenge had strengthened him for the journey.

Perseverance in faith is like the goat's climb—each step, no matter how difficult, brings us closer to the rewards God has prepared for us.

Biblical Examples of Perseverance

The Bible is filled with examples of those who persevered in faith. Paul endured shipwrecks, imprisonments, and persecution but remained steadfast in his mission to spread the Gospel. In 2 Timothy 4:7, he declared, "I have fought the good fight, I have finished the race, I have kept the faith."

Job's story also illustrates perseverance. Despite losing everything, he held onto his faith, saying, "Though He slay me, yet will I trust Him" (Job 13:15 NKJV). God restored Job's fortunes, demonstrating His faithfulness to those who endure.

The Fruit of Perseverance

Perseverance produces spiritual growth and maturity. James 1:3-4 says, "Knowing that the testing of your faith produces patience. But let patience have its perfect work, that you may be perfect and complete, lacking nothing." Challenges refine us, strengthening our character and deepening our reliance on God.

Hebrews 12:1-2 encourages us to run the race with endurance, "looking unto Jesus, the author and finisher of our faith." Keeping our focus on Christ enables us to persevere through trials and remain faithful to God's call.

Reflection Questions

In what areas of your life do you need to persevere and trust in God's timing?

_____

_____

_____

How have past challenges strengthened your faith and character?

_____

_____

_____

What steps can you take to remain steadfast in your walk with God during difficult times?

_____

_____

_____

Prayer Prompt

Lord, thank You for the strength to persevere through life's challenges. Teach me to rely on Your promises and to trust in Your timing. Help me to remain steadfast in faith, knowing that You are always with me and that my efforts will bear fruit in Your perfect plan. Amen.

Day 35: God's Love as Our Foundation

The Power of God's Love

God's love is the unshakable foundation of our lives. 1 John 4:16 declares, "And we have known and believed the love that God has for us. God is love, and he who abides in love abides in God, and God in him." His love gives us strength, security, and purpose.

Romans 8:38-39 assures us, "For I am persuaded that neither death nor life, nor angels nor principalities nor powers, nor things present nor things to come, nor height nor depth, nor any other created thing, shall be able to separate us from the love of God which is in Christ Jesus our Lord."

Parable: The Builder's Cornerstone

A builder was constructing a great cathedral. He began with a solid cornerstone, carefully placing it as the foundation of the entire structure. When others questioned why he spent so much time on a single stone, the builder explained, "If the cornerstone is not secure, the entire building will crumble."

Years later, the cathedral stood tall and unshaken, even through storms and earthquakes, because it was built on a firm foundation.

God's love is our cornerstone. When we build our lives on His love, we are unshaken by life's storms and challenges, standing firm in His promises.

Living in God's Love

Living in God's love transforms the way we see ourselves and others. 1 John 4:19 reminds us, "We love Him because He first loved us." Embracing God's love allows us to extend grace, forgiveness, and compassion to those around us.

Jesus emphasized this in John 13:34-35: "A new commandment I give to you, that you love one another; as I have loved you, that you also love one another. By this all will know that you are My disciples, if you have love for one another." Love is the hallmark of a life grounded in Christ.

The Security of God's Love

God's love provides security and peace in a world filled with uncertainty. Psalm 36:7 declares, "How precious is Your lovingkindness, O God! Therefore the children of men put their trust under the shadow of Your wings." His love is a refuge, offering comfort and strength no matter our circumstances.

Paul's prayer in Ephesians 3:17-19 captures the depth of God's love: "That Christ may dwell in your hearts through faith; that you, being rooted and grounded in love, may be able to comprehend with all the saints what is the width and length and depth and height—to know the love of Christ which passes knowledge." Knowing God's love empowers us to live boldly and purposefully.

Reflection Questions

How has God's love been a foundation of strength and security in your life?

_____

_____

_____

In what ways can you reflect God's love to those around you?

_____

_____

_____

How can living in God's love transform your perspective on challenges and relationships?

_____

_____

_____

Prayer Prompt

Lord, thank You for Your unshakable love that is the foundation of my life. Teach me to build my faith on Your love and to reflect it in my actions and relationships. Help me to stand firm in Your promises, knowing that nothing can separate me from Your love. Amen.

Day 36: God's Purpose in Every Season

Trusting God's Timing

Every season of life serves a purpose in God's plan. Ecclesiastes 3:1 reminds us, "To everything there is a season, a time for every purpose under heaven." Trusting God's timing allows us to see His hand at work, even in periods of waiting or difficulty.

Romans 8:28 assures us, "And we know that all things work together for good to those who love God, to those who are the called according to His purpose." God weaves every experience into His greater plan for our lives.

Parable: The Potter's Wheel

A potter carefully shaped a lump of clay on his wheel, pressing and molding it with great care. Impatient, the clay cried out, "Why must I endure this stretching and spinning? Can't you finish me already?"

The potter replied, "The process is necessary. If I rush, the vessel will be weak and unable to fulfill its purpose. Trust that I am creating something beautiful."

When the work was complete, the clay became a strong and elegant vessel, ready to be used. Like the potter, God shapes us through every season, preparing us for His purpose in His perfect time.

God's Purpose in the Bible

Joseph's life is a powerful example of God's purpose unfolding through seasons of trial and triumph. Sold into slavery by his brothers, Joseph endured years of hardship before rising to a position of leadership in Egypt. Reflecting on his journey, he told his brothers, "You meant evil against me; but God meant it for good" (Genesis 50:20 NKJV). Joseph's faith in God's purpose sustained him through every challenge.

Similarly, Esther's season of preparation led to her pivotal role in saving her people. Mordecai reminded her, "Yet who knows whether you have come to the kingdom for such a time as this?" (Esther 4:14 NKJV). Her courage and obedience fulfilled God's plan for her life.

Finding Joy in Every Season

God calls us to embrace each season with faith and gratitude. James 1:2-4 encourages, "My brethren, count it all joy when you fall into various trials, knowing that the testing of your faith produces patience. But let patience have its perfect work, that you may be perfect and complete, lacking nothing." Challenges refine us and prepare us for God's purposes.

Isaiah 40:31 reminds us that waiting on God renews our strength: "But those who wait on the Lord shall renew their strength; they shall mount up with wings like eagles, they shall run and not be weary, they shall walk and not faint." Trusting God's timing brings peace and confidence in His plan.

Reflection Questions

How can you trust God's purpose in the season you are currently experiencing?

_____

_____

_____

What lessons or growth have you gained from past seasons of waiting or trial?

_____

_____

_____

How can you use your current season to glorify God and prepare for His next step?

_____

_____

_____

Prayer Prompt

Lord, thank You for the purpose You have for every season of my life. Teach me to trust in Your timing and to embrace each moment with faith and gratitude. Help me to see Your hand at work and to walk confidently in the plans You have for me. Amen.

Day 37: The Power of Forgiveness

God's Call to Forgive

Forgiveness is a command that brings freedom and healing. Matthew 6:14-15 teaches, "For if you forgive men their trespasses, your heavenly Father will also forgive you. But if you do not forgive men their trespasses, neither will your Father forgive your trespasses." Forgiveness reflects God's grace in our lives.

Ephesians 4:32 encourages, "And be kind to one another, tenderhearted, forgiving one another, even as God in Christ forgave you." Forgiving others mirrors the forgiveness we have received from God.

Parable: The Two Debtors

Two men owed a wealthy merchant a great deal of money. One owed a small amount, while the other owed a massive sum. The merchant forgave both debts completely. The man with the smaller debt walked away unchanged, but the one with the larger debt wept with gratitude and vowed to live a life of generosity.

The merchant later said, "The one who understands the weight of forgiveness shows it in how they live."

Similarly, when we grasp the depth of God's forgiveness toward us, it transforms how we extend grace to others. Forgiveness is not just a gift we receive—it's one we are called to give.

Biblical Examples of Forgiveness

The Bible offers powerful stories of forgiveness. Joseph forgave his brothers for selling him into slavery, saying, "Do not be afraid; for am I in the place of God? You meant evil against me; but God meant it for good" (Genesis 50:19-20 NKJV). His forgiveness allowed healing and reconciliation to take place.

Jesus demonstrated ultimate forgiveness on the cross, saying, "Father, forgive them, for they do not know what they do" (Luke 23:34 NKJV). His example reminds us that forgiveness is not about excusing wrongs but releasing ourselves from bitterness and choosing love.

The Freedom of Forgiveness

Forgiveness brings freedom to our hearts and relationships. Colossians 3:13 urges, "Bear with each other and forgive one another if any of you has a grievance against someone. Forgive as the Lord forgave you." Letting go of resentment allows God's peace to reign in our lives.

Forgiveness also creates space for God's healing. Isaiah 1:18 invites us, "Though your sins are like scarlet, they shall be as white as snow." Just as God cleanses us, forgiving others restores our hearts and draws us closer to Him.

Reflection Questions

Who in your life do you need to forgive, and how can you take a step toward healing?

_____

_____

_____

How does understanding God's forgiveness toward you inspire you to forgive others?

_____

_____

_____

What benefits have you experienced when you chose to release resentment and offer forgiveness?

_____

_____

_____

Prayer Prompt

Lord, thank You for forgiving me and setting me free from my sins. Teach me to extend the same grace to others, even when it feels difficult. Help me to let go of bitterness and to walk in the freedom and peace that forgiveness brings. Amen.

Day 38: Living with Purpose

God's Plan for Our Lives

Each of us is created with a unique purpose designed by God. Jeremiah 29:11 reminds us, "For I know the plans I have for you, says the Lord, plans to prosper you and not to harm you, plans to give you hope and a future." Walking in God's purpose brings fulfillment and direction.

Ephesians 2:10 declares, "For we are His workmanship, created in Christ Jesus for good works, which God prepared beforehand that we should walk in them." God has equipped us with gifts and opportunities to fulfill His plan for our lives.

Parable: The Unused Key

A young locksmith received a beautiful, intricate key as a gift from his mentor. However, he didn't know what it unlocked, so he set it aside, thinking it had no use. Years later, he discovered an old chest in his mentor's workshop. To his surprise, the key fit perfectly, revealing treasures that had been waiting for him all along.

The locksmith realized the key had value all along—he just hadn't known its purpose.

Like the key, God has given each of us unique gifts and purposes. When we seek Him and trust His timing, we discover how those gifts unlock the potential He has placed within us.

Finding Purpose in God's Word

The Bible guides us in discovering and fulfilling our purpose. Psalm 37:23 assures us, "The steps of a good man are ordered by the Lord, and He delights in his way." Seeking God through Scripture and prayer helps us align our goals with His will.

Esther's life illustrates this beautifully. Though she initially hesitated to act, her cousin Mordecai reminded her, "Who knows whether you have come to the kingdom for such a time as this?" (Esther 4:14 NKJV). Her obedience fulfilled God's plan to save her people.

Living Intentionally

Fulfilling God's purpose requires intentionality and trust. Proverbs 16:3 advises, "Commit your works to the Lord, and your thoughts will be established." When we surrender our plans to God, He directs our paths and reveals His purpose.

Paul's life demonstrates purposeful living. In Acts 20:24, he declared, "But none of these things move me, nor do I count my life dear to myself, so that I may finish my race with joy, and the ministry which I received from the Lord Jesus." His unwavering focus on God's mission inspires us to live with dedication and passion.

Reflection Questions

What gifts and talents has God given you to fulfill His purpose?

_____
_____
_____

How can you seek God's guidance to discover or deepen your sense of purpose?

_____
_____
_____

In what ways can you live more intentionally to align your daily life with God's plan?

_____
_____
_____

Prayer Prompt

Lord, thank You for creating me with a purpose and for guiding my steps. Teach me to seek Your will and to trust in Your plan for my life. Help me to use my gifts for Your glory and to live intentionally, fulfilling the mission You have given me. Amen.

Day 39: The Power of Faithfulness

Faithfulness Reflects God's Character

Faithfulness is a key attribute of God, and He calls us to reflect it in our lives. Lamentations 3:22-23 reminds us, "Through the Lord's mercies we are not consumed, because His compassions fail not. They are new every morning; great is Your faithfulness." Living faithfully honors God and builds trust in our relationships.

1 Corinthians 4:2 emphasizes, "Moreover it is required in stewards that one be found faithful." Faithfulness in our responsibilities, relationships, and faith walk brings glory to God.

Parable: The Candle Keeper

In a small village, a man was tasked with keeping the lighthouse candle burning every night. Though the task seemed insignificant, he remained faithful, tending to the flame without fail. One stormy night, a ship veered dangerously close to the rocks. The captain later told the man, "Your light saved us."

The candle keeper realized that his consistent effort had made a difference. Like the keeper, our faithfulness, even in small tasks, can have a profound impact on others and reflect God's steadfast love.

Biblical Examples of Faithfulness

Throughout Scripture, we see examples of faithfulness. Noah obeyed God's command to build the ark, despite the ridicule of others. His steadfastness saved his family and preserved God's creation (Genesis 6:22).

Ruth's loyalty to Naomi is another example. She declared, "Where you go, I will go; and where you lodge, I will lodge" (Ruth 1:16 NKJV). Her faithfulness led to her becoming part of God's redemptive plan through the lineage of Jesus.

The Rewards of Faithfulness

Faithfulness brings blessings and fulfills God's purposes. In Matthew 25:21, Jesus says, "Well done, good and faithful servant; you were faithful over a few things, I will make you ruler over many things. Enter into the joy of your lord." Remaining faithful in small responsibilities prepares us for greater opportunities in God's kingdom.

Faithfulness also strengthens our relationship with God. Galatians 6:9 encourages, "And let us not grow weary while doing good, for in due season we shall reap if we do not lose heart." Trusting God's timing motivates us to persevere with faith and consistency.

Reflection Questions

In what areas of your life do you need to cultivate greater faithfulness?

_____

_____

_____

How has your faithfulness to God and others impacted your relationships?

_____
_____
_____

What steps can you take to remain steadfast in your daily walk with God?

_____
_____
_____

Prayer Prompt

Lord, thank You for Your unwavering faithfulness to me. Teach me to reflect Your character through my actions and to remain steadfast in every responsibility. Help me to trust in Your timing and to honor You through my faithfulness in both small and great tasks. Amen.

Day 40: The Power of Generosity

God's Call to Generosity

Generosity reflects the heart of God, who gives abundantly to His children. Luke 6:38 teaches, "Give, and it will be given to you: good measure, pressed down, shaken together, and running over will be put into your bosom. For with the same measure that you use, it will be measured back to you." Giving is an act of trust and worship that invites God's blessings into our lives.

Proverbs 11:25 assures us, "The generous soul will be made rich, and he who waters will also be watered himself." Generosity not only blesses others but also renews our spirits.

Parable: The Overflowing Jar

A farmer kept a jar of seeds to plant each spring. One year, he felt hesitant to use too many seeds, fearing a poor harvest. Instead, his neighbor generously scattered her seeds across her field, trusting that the land would yield abundantly.

When harvest time came, the farmer's field was sparse, while his neighbor's field was overflowing. The farmer realized, "The more you give, the more you receive."

Generosity is like scattering seeds—it multiplies blessings and creates opportunities for growth, both for us and for those we give to.

Biblical Examples of Generosity

The Bible provides many examples of generosity. The widow in Zarephath gave her last bit of flour and oil to Elijah, trusting God's promise. Her obedience and generosity led to a miracle: her jar of flour and jug of oil never ran dry (1 Kings 17:8-16).

Jesus highlighted the widow who gave two small coins at the temple. He said, "Truly I tell you, this poor widow has put in more than all the others. All these people gave their gifts out of their wealth; but she out of her poverty put in all she had to live on" (Luke 21:3-4 NIV). Her heart of generosity demonstrated faith and devotion.

The Joy of Giving

Generosity brings joy and strengthens our connection with God and others. Acts 20:35 reminds us, "It is more blessed to give than to receive." Giving shifts our focus from ourselves to God's kingdom, aligning us with His purpose.

Paul encourages cheerful giving in 2 Corinthians 9:7: "So let each one give as he purposes in his heart, not grudgingly or of necessity; for God loves a cheerful giver." When we give willingly, we experience the joy and fulfillment that come from honoring God with our resources.

Reflection Questions

How can you cultivate a heart of generosity in your daily life?

_____

_____

_____

In what ways have you experienced God's blessings through giving to others?

_____
_____
_____

How can you use your resources to advance God's kingdom and bless those in need?

_____
_____
_____

Prayer Prompt

Lord, thank You for Your abundant generosity in my life. Teach me to give with a cheerful heart and to trust in Your provision. Help me to use the blessings You have given me to bless others and to bring glory to Your name. Amen.

Day 41: God's Peace in Waiting

The Challenge of Waiting

Waiting is one of life's most difficult tests, but God's peace sustains us in the process. Isaiah 40:31 promises, "But those who wait on the Lord shall renew their strength; they shall mount up with wings like eagles, they shall run and not be weary, they shall walk and not faint." Trusting in God's timing allows us to experience His peace even in uncertainty.

Psalm 27:14 encourages, "Wait on the Lord; be of good courage, and He shall strengthen your heart; wait, I say, on the Lord!" God's presence gives us strength and patience as we wait for His plans to unfold.

Parable: The Weaver's Loom

A young apprentice worked under a skilled weaver who created intricate tapestries. The apprentice was eager to see the final design, but all he could see while weaving were the messy, tangled threads on the back of the tapestry.

Impatient, he asked the master, "Why does it look so chaotic? Is this really leading to something beautiful?"

The weaver smiled and turned the loom, revealing a stunning design. "What seemed like chaos," he said, "was part of the process for creating something extraordinary."

Waiting on God is like weaving a tapestry—we often see only the tangled threads, but God sees the completed masterpiece. Trusting His timing brings peace as we await the beauty He is creating in our lives.

Biblical Examples of Waiting

The Bible is filled with stories of individuals who waited on God's timing. Abraham and Sarah waited 25 years for the fulfillment of God's promise of a son. Their journey reminds us that God's delays are not His denials (Genesis 21:1-2).

David was anointed as king but spent years in the wilderness before ascending the throne. During this time, he wrote many Psalms that reflected his trust in God's timing. Psalm 37:7 encourages, "Rest in the Lord, and wait patiently for Him."

Finding Peace in the Wait

Waiting is an opportunity to deepen our faith and trust in God. Philippians 4:6-7 reminds us, "Be anxious for nothing, but in everything by prayer and supplication, with thanksgiving, let your requests be made known to God; and the peace of God, which surpasses all understanding, will guard your hearts and minds through Christ Jesus."

When we surrender our timelines to God, we experience peace that comes from knowing He is in control. Proverbs 3:5-6 encourages, "Trust in the Lord with all your heart, and lean not on your own understanding; in all your ways acknowledge Him, and He shall direct your paths."

Reflection Questions

How can you trust God more fully in seasons of waiting?

_____

_____

_____

In what ways has waiting on God strengthened your faith and character?

_____

_____

_____

How can you encourage others who are waiting for God's timing in their lives?

_____

_____

_____

Prayer Prompt

Lord, thank You for being with me in every season of waiting. Teach me to trust in Your timing and to rest in Your promises. Help me to find peace in Your presence and to grow in faith as I wait for Your plans to unfold. Amen.

Day 42: The Beauty of Humility

God's Call to Humility

Humility is essential for a life that honors God. James 4:10 encourages us, "Humble yourselves in the sight of the Lord, and He will lift you up." Living with humility allows us to recognize our dependence on God and opens the door for His grace to work in our lives.

Philippians 2:3-4 reminds us, "Let nothing be done through selfish ambition or conceit, but in lowliness of mind let each esteem others better than himself. Let each of you look out not only for his own interests, but also for the interests of others." Humility reflects the character of Christ and strengthens our relationships.

Parable: The Empty Cup

A wise teacher welcomed a proud student who claimed to know everything. The teacher offered the student tea, but as he poured, the cup overflowed. Alarmed, the student exclaimed, "The cup is full! No more can fit!"

The teacher replied, "Exactly. Like this cup, your mind is too full to learn anything new. To gain wisdom, you must first empty yourself of pride."

Humility is like an empty cup—it creates space for God to pour His wisdom, grace, and purpose into our lives. When we let go of pride, we open ourselves to His transforming work.

Christ's Example of Humility

Jesus is the ultimate example of humility. Philippians 2:5-7 teaches, "Let this mind be in you which was also in Christ Jesus, who, being in the form of God, did not consider it robbery to be equal with God, but made Himself of no reputation, taking the form of a bondservant." His willingness to serve and sacrifice for others reveals the power of humility.

In John 13, Jesus washed His disciples' feet, an act of humility and love. He told them, "If I then, your Lord and Teacher, have washed your feet, you also ought to wash one another's feet" (John 13:14 NKJV). His example reminds us that true greatness comes from serving others.

The Blessings of Humility

God promises to bless those who walk in humility. Proverbs 22:4 declares, "By humility and the fear of the Lord are riches and honor and life." Humility positions us to receive God's grace and favor.

1 Peter 5:6-7 encourages, "Therefore humble yourselves under the mighty hand of God, that He may exalt you in due time, casting all your care upon Him, for He cares for you." When we surrender our pride and trust in God, He lifts us up in His perfect timing.

Reflection Questions

How can you cultivate humility in your daily life and relationships?

_____

_____

_____

In what areas do you need to let go of pride and trust in God's grace?

_____

_____

_____

How does Christ's example of humility inspire you to serve others?

_____

_____

_____

Prayer Prompt

Lord, thank You for teaching me the beauty of humility. Help me to let go of pride and to embrace a heart of service and dependence on You. Teach me to follow Christ's example of humility, honoring You in all that I do. Amen.

Day 43: The Gift of Contentment

Finding Contentment in God

Contentment is a gift that comes from trusting in God's provision and plan for our lives. Philippians 4:11-12 reminds us, "Not that I speak in regard to need, for I have learned in whatever state I am, to be content: I know how to be abased, and I know how to abound. Everywhere and in all things I have learned both to be full and to be hungry, both to abound and to suffer need."

Hebrews 13:5 encourages, "Let your conduct be without covetousness; be content with such things as you have. For He Himself has said, 'I will never leave you nor forsake you.'" Trusting in God's presence and promises brings true peace and satisfaction.

Parable: The Traveler and the Treasure

A traveler came across two villagers. One complained about his small house, wishing for riches and luxury. The other, with the same modest house, smiled as he enjoyed a simple meal. Curious, the traveler asked, "Why are you so content with so little?"

The villager replied, "I focus on what I have rather than what I lack. Each day is a treasure when you choose to see it."

Contentment is like seeing treasure in the ordinary. When we focus on God's blessings instead of what we lack, we discover the joy and peace He provides in every season.

Biblical Examples of Contentment

Paul exemplified contentment through his faith in God. Despite facing imprisonment, persecution, and hardship, he declared, "I can do all things through Christ who strengthens me" (Philippians 4:13). His trust in God's provision allowed him to remain steadfast, regardless of his circumstances.

The widow of Zarephath also demonstrated contentment when Elijah asked her to make him a meal with her last bit of flour and oil. She obeyed, trusting God's promise, and her resources never ran out (1 Kings 17:12-16). Her story reminds us that contentment flows from faith in God's provision.

Cultivating Contentment

Contentment requires a shift in perspective. 1 Timothy 6:6-7 teaches, "Now godliness with contentment is great gain. For we brought nothing into this world, and it is certain we can carry nothing out." Recognizing the temporary nature of material things helps us focus on eternal blessings.

Gratitude also fosters contentment. Psalm 103:2 encourages, "Bless the Lord, O my soul, and forget not all His benefits." Reflecting on God's faithfulness reminds us of His abundant provision and keeps our hearts at peace.

Reflection Questions

What blessings in your life can you focus on to cultivate contentment?

_____
_____
_____

In what areas do you struggle with comparison or dissatisfaction, and how can you surrender those feelings to God?

_____
_____
_____

How can you practice gratitude daily to grow in contentment?

_____
_____
_____

Prayer Prompt

Lord, thank You for the gift of contentment that comes from trusting in You. Teach me to focus on Your blessings and to let go of dissatisfaction and comparison. Help me to find joy in Your presence and peace in every season of life. Amen.

Day 44: God's Strength in Community

The Importance of Fellowship

God created us to thrive in relationships with others. Ecclesiastes 4:9-10 reminds us, "Two are better than one, because they have a good reward for their labor. For if they fall, one will lift up his companion." Community provides strength, encouragement, and support in our faith journey.

Hebrews 10:24-25 urges, "And let us consider one another in order to stir up love and good works, not forsaking the assembling of ourselves together, as is the manner of some, but exhorting one another." Fellowship strengthens our connection to God and to one another.

Parable: The Rope Bridge

A group of travelers reached a canyon with a fragile-looking rope bridge. Hesitant to cross, one traveler suggested, "Let's hold the ropes together to keep it steady." Linking arms and moving as one, they crossed the bridge safely.

One traveler said, "Alone, I might not have made it, but together we were strong."

Community is like that—when we stand together, we overcome challenges that might feel insurmountable on our own. Fellowship strengthens our faith and helps us navigate life's uncertainties with courage.

Biblical Examples of Community

The early church in Acts is a powerful example of the strength of community. Acts 2:44-47 describes, "Now all who believed were together, and had all things in common, and sold their possessions and goods, and divided them among all, as anyone had need." Their unity and generosity reflected God's love and drew others to the faith.

Jesus Himself modeled the importance of community by surrounding Himself with disciples. He taught, served, and prayed with them, demonstrating the power of shared faith and relationships.

Living in Godly Community

Being part of a godly community helps us grow in faith and character. Proverbs 27:17 teaches, "As iron sharpens iron, so a man sharpens the countenance of his friend." Accountability and encouragement from others strengthen our walk with God.

Fellowship also reminds us of our shared purpose in Christ. 1 Corinthians 12:12-14 emphasizes, "For as the body is one and has many members, but all the members of that one body, being many, are one body, so also is Christ." Each person plays a vital role in the body of Christ, contributing to its unity and mission.

Reflection Questions

How has being part of a faith community strengthened your relationship with God?

_____

_____

_____

In what ways can you contribute to building up and encouraging others in your community?

_____

_____

_____

How can you deepen your connections with others to grow in faith together?

_____

_____

_____

Prayer Prompt

Lord, thank You for the gift of community and the strength it provides. Teach me to build meaningful relationships that honor You and encourage others. Help me to serve, love, and uplift those around me so that we may grow together in faith and unity. Amen.

Day 45: The Power of Gratitude

Gratitude as a Foundation of Faith

Gratitude shifts our perspective and deepens our faith. 1 Thessalonians 5:18 encourages, "In everything give thanks; for this is the will of God in Christ Jesus for you." Choosing to be thankful, even in challenging times, reflects our trust in God's goodness and provision.

Psalm 100:4 reminds us, "Enter into His gates with thanksgiving, and into His courts with praise. Be thankful to Him, and bless His name." Gratitude is not just an emotion—it is an act of worship.

Parable: The Two Farmers

Two farmers faced a severe drought. One complained daily about the lack of rain, while the other gave thanks for each morning and continued preparing his field. When the rains finally came, the thankful farmer's field was ready for planting, while the other farmer had wasted precious time.

The second farmer remarked, "Gratitude keeps you ready for the blessings that are yet to come."

Gratitude, like the prepared field, positions us to receive God's blessings with open hearts. It changes our focus from scarcity to abundance, allowing us to see His provision in every season.

Gratitude in Trials

Giving thanks during difficulties is not easy, but it is transformative. James 1:2-3 encourages, "My brethren, count it all joy when you fall into various trials, knowing that the testing of your faith produces patience." Gratitude in trials helps us see God's hand at work, even when the outcome is unclear.

Paul and Silas demonstrated this in Acts 16:25. While imprisoned, they sang hymns of praise to God. Their gratitude and worship led to a miraculous prison break, reminding us that gratitude has the power to change not only our circumstances but also our hearts.

Living a Life of Gratitude

Gratitude is a daily practice that enriches our relationship with God and others. Colossians 3:15 says, "And let the peace of God rule in your hearts, to which also you were called in one body; and be thankful." Thankfulness cultivates peace, joy, and contentment, even in the midst of life's challenges.

Choosing gratitude also blesses those around us. By expressing thankfulness to others, we reflect God's love and encourage a spirit of kindness and generosity.

Reflection Questions

How can you cultivate a habit of gratitude in your daily life, even in difficult times?

_____

_____

_____

In what ways has gratitude deepened your trust in God and strengthened your faith?

_____

_____

_____

How can you use your thankfulness to encourage and bless others?

_____

_____

_____

Prayer Prompt

Lord, thank You for Your abundant blessings and unwavering faithfulness. Teach me to cultivate a heart of gratitude, even in times of trial. Help me to focus on Your goodness and to reflect Your love and kindness to others through my thankfulness. Amen.

Day 46: The Strength of Integrity

Living a Life of Integrity

Integrity is living in alignment with God's truth and principles, even when no one is watching. Proverbs 10:9 declares, "He who walks with integrity walks securely, but he who perverts his ways will become known." Integrity brings security and trust, allowing us to honor God in every aspect of our lives.

Psalm 41:12 reminds us, "As for me, You uphold me in my integrity, and set me before Your face forever." When we commit to living uprightly, God's favor and presence sustain us.

Parable: The Hidden Stone

A sculptor worked on a magnificent statue, spending hours perfecting the details that would be hidden within the base. A passerby asked, "Why waste time on something no one will see?"

The sculptor replied, "Integrity is doing what's right, even when it's unseen. The hidden work ensures the entire statue will stand strong."

Like the sculptor, our unseen choices shape the strength of our character. Integrity is about honoring God and staying true to His principles, regardless of whether anyone else notices.

Biblical Examples of Integrity

Joseph is a powerful example of integrity. Despite being falsely accused by Potiphar's wife, he refused to compromise his values, saying, "How then can I do this great wickedness, and sin against God?" (Genesis 39:9

NKJV). His commitment to integrity ultimately led to his rise to power in Egypt.

Daniel also demonstrated integrity when he continued praying to God despite a decree that made it punishable by death. His faithfulness resulted in God's miraculous protection in the lions' den (Daniel 6:10-23). Both Joseph and Daniel remind us that integrity invites God's favor and protection.

The Blessings of Integrity

Integrity builds trust and strengthens our relationships. Proverbs 11:3 teaches, "The integrity of the upright will guide them, but the perversity of the unfaithful will destroy them." Living with integrity allows us to make decisions that honor God and foster respect from others.

Integrity also brings peace. Isaiah 32:17 declares, "The work of righteousness will be peace, and the effect of righteousness, quietness and assurance forever." A life grounded in God's truth eliminates the need for deception or fear, replacing it with confidence and assurance.

Reflection Questions

In what areas of your life do you need to strengthen your commitment to integrity?

_____

_____

_____

How has living with integrity impacted your relationship with God and others?

_____

_____

_____

What steps can you take to ensure your daily decisions align with God's principles?

_____

_____

_____

Prayer Prompt

Lord, thank You for being my example of perfect integrity. Teach me to walk uprightly and to honor You in every decision, both seen and unseen. Help me to live with courage and faithfulness, trusting in Your guidance and strength. Amen.

Day 47: The Power of Perseverance

Endurance Through Faith

Perseverance is a vital quality for fulfilling God's purposes. Galatians 6:9 encourages, "And let us not grow weary while doing good, for in due season we shall reap if we do not lose heart." Trusting in God's promises gives us the strength to endure life's challenges.

James 1:12 reminds us, "Blessed is the man who endures temptation; for when he has been approved, he will receive the crown of life which the Lord has promised to those who love Him." Endurance is not only about surviving trials but thriving through them with faith.

Parable: The Stone Cutter

A stonecutter struck a massive boulder repeatedly, day after day, without seeing any results. Passersby mocked him, asking, "Why waste your effort on something that won't break?"

The stonecutter replied, "Each strike is progress, even if I don't see it yet."

On the hundredth strike, the boulder split in two. The stonecutter explained, "It wasn't the final blow that did it, but the perseverance behind every strike."

Perseverance in faith is like the stonecutter's effort. Each prayer, step of obedience, and act of trust brings us closer to God's breakthrough, even when progress seems invisible.

Biblical Examples of Perseverance

The Bible is filled with stories of perseverance. Noah worked on the ark for decades, enduring ridicule, but his faithfulness led to the preservation of life (Genesis 6:13-22). His example reminds us that perseverance often requires trust in God's unseen plan.

Paul also demonstrated remarkable endurance. Despite facing shipwrecks, beatings, and imprisonments, he declared, "I have fought the good fight, I have finished the race, I have kept the faith" (2 Timothy 4:7). His perseverance inspires us to remain faithful, no matter the obstacles.

The Reward of Perseverance

Perseverance produces spiritual growth and maturity. James 1:2-4 teaches, "Count it all joy when you fall into various trials, knowing that the testing of your faith produces patience. But let patience have its perfect work, that you may be perfect and complete, lacking nothing." Challenges refine us and strengthen our dependence on God.

Hebrews 12:1-2 urges us to run the race with endurance, "looking unto Jesus, the author and finisher of our faith." Keeping our focus on Christ gives us the strength to persevere and fulfill the purpose He has set before us.

Reflection Questions

What challenges in your life require perseverance and trust in God's promises?

_____

_____

_____

How can you focus on God's faithfulness to strengthen your endurance?

_____

_____

_____

In what ways has perseverance in the past deepened your faith and character?

_____

_____

_____

Prayer Prompt

Lord, thank You for being my strength in times of trial. Teach me to persevere with faith and confidence in Your promises. Help me to trust in Your timing and to remain steadfast in the race You have set before me, knowing that You are always with me. Amen.

Day 48: The Beauty of Compassion

God's Call to Compassion

Compassion reflects the heart of God and draws us closer to His character. Colossians 3:12 encourages, "Therefore, as God's chosen people, holy and dearly loved, clothe yourselves with compassion, kindness, humility, gentleness, and patience." Showing compassion demonstrates God's love in action.

Psalm 103:13 reminds us, "As a father has compassion on his children, so the Lord has compassion on those who fear Him." God's compassion toward us inspires us to extend the same care and kindness to others.

Parable: The Wounded Sparrow

A man walking through the woods came across a sparrow with a broken wing. While others passed it by, he stopped, gently picked it up, and brought it to his home. Over time, he nursed the sparrow back to health and released it into the wild.

A year later, the man found his garden filled with birdsong, the sparrow among them. Its return reminded him that small acts of compassion have a lasting impact.

Like the man with the sparrow, our compassionate actions may seem small, but they can make a significant difference in someone's life, reflecting God's care and love.

Biblical Examples of Compassion

Jesus exemplified compassion throughout His ministry. When He saw the crowds, He was moved with compassion for them, "because they were weary and scattered, like sheep having no shepherd" (Matthew 9:36 NKJV). His compassion led Him to heal the sick, feed the hungry, and preach hope to the lost.

The Good Samaritan also demonstrated compassion by helping a man who had been beaten and left for dead. While others passed by, the Samaritan stopped, cared for the man's wounds, and ensured his safety (Luke 10:25-37). His story reminds us that true compassion transcends social or cultural boundaries.

Living with Compassion

Compassion requires us to see others through God's eyes and act on their behalf. 1 John 3:17 asks, "But whoever has this world's goods, and sees his brother in need, and shuts up his heart from him, how does the love of God abide in him?" Compassion involves not only feeling for others but also taking steps to meet their needs.

Micah 6:8 challenges us to "act justly and to love mercy and to walk humbly with your God." Compassionate living reflects God's mercy and inspires others to experience His love.

Reflection Questions

How can you practice compassion in your daily life?

_____

_____

_____

In what ways has God's compassion toward you inspired you to care for others?

_____

_____

_____

What small act of kindness can you do this week to make a difference for someone in need?

_____

_____

_____

Prayer Prompt

Lord, thank You for Your compassion and mercy in my life. Teach me to see others through Your eyes and to respond to their needs with kindness and love. Help me to reflect Your heart through acts of compassion and to bring hope to those around me. Amen.

Day 49: The Blessing of Rest

God's Design for Rest

Rest is a gift from God that restores our bodies, minds, and spirits. Matthew 11:28 invites us, "Come to Me, all you who labor and are heavy laden, and I will give you rest." God designed rest not only for physical renewal but also for spiritual restoration.

Exodus 20:8-10 commands, "Remember the Sabbath day, to keep it holy. Six days you shall labor and do all your work, but the seventh day is the Sabbath of the Lord your God." Honoring rest as God intended allows us to reflect on His provision and trust in His care.

Parable: The Lumberjack's Axe

A lumberjack worked tirelessly every day, cutting down trees to provide for his family. Over time, his axe became dull, but he refused to take a break to sharpen it, fearing he would fall behind. His productivity dwindled, and frustration grew.

One day, an old woodsman advised, "Take time to sharpen your axe, and you'll accomplish more with less effort." Reluctantly, the lumberjack paused to sharpen his tool. To his amazement, he finished his work faster and with less strain.

Rest is like sharpening the axe. It may feel counterproductive, but it renews our strength and allows us to work more effectively in God's purpose.

Biblical Examples of Rest

God Himself modeled rest after creating the world. Genesis 2:2 says, "And on the seventh day God ended His work which He had done, and He rested on the seventh day from all His work which He had done." If the Creator of the universe valued rest, how much more should we?

Jesus also prioritized rest during His ministry. Mark 6:31 recounts, "And He said to them, 'Come aside by yourselves to a deserted place and rest a while.'" Despite the demands of the crowds, Jesus knew the importance of stepping away to recharge and reconnect with God.

The Renewal of Rest

Rest is not just about physical recovery—it is an act of faith. Psalm 23:2-3 reminds us, "He makes me to lie down in green pastures; He leads me beside the still waters. He restores my soul." Trusting God enough to rest acknowledges that He is in control and we can rely on Him.

Isaiah 40:29-31 encourages, "He gives power to the weak, and to those who have no might He increases strength...those who wait on the Lord shall renew their strength." Rest allows us to find renewed strength and clarity to fulfill God's calling.

Reflection Questions

How can you prioritize rest in your life without feeling guilty or unproductive?

_____

_____

_____

In what ways does rest help you connect more deeply with God and His purpose for you?

_____

_____

_____

What steps can you take to incorporate regular physical and spiritual rest into your routine?

_____

_____

_____

Prayer Prompt

Lord, thank You for the gift of rest that renews my strength and deepens my trust in You. Teach me to honor the rhythms of rest You have created and to rely on Your provision rather than my own efforts. Help me to find peace and restoration in Your presence. Amen.

Day 50: The Gift of Hope

Hope Anchored in God

Hope is the confident expectation of God's promises, even when circumstances seem uncertain. Hebrews 6:19 reminds us, "This hope we have as an anchor of the soul, both sure and steadfast." God's hope sustains us through life's storms, giving us strength and peace.

Romans 15:13 encourages, "Now may the God of hope fill you with all joy and peace in believing, that you may abound in hope by the power of the Holy Spirit." True hope comes from trusting in God's faithfulness and love.

Parable: The Sapling in the Storm

A young sapling stood in the middle of a field, exposed to strong winds and heavy rains. Nearby, an old oak tree told it, "Bend with the storm, and trust your roots to hold you firm."

Though battered, the sapling survived the storm. When the skies cleared, its roots had grown deeper, anchoring it more securely than before.

Like the sapling, hope in God anchors us during life's storms. It strengthens us to endure trials, knowing that His promises and presence will hold us firm no matter what we face.

Biblical Examples of Hope

The Bible offers powerful examples of hope. Abraham hoped against all odds, trusting God's promise of a son despite his advanced age. Romans 4:18 says, "Who, contrary to hope, in hope believed." His unwavering faith reminds us that God's promises never fail.

Job also clung to hope despite losing everything. He declared, "For I know that my Redeemer lives, and He shall stand at last on the earth" (Job 19:25 NKJV). Job's hope in God's justice and restoration carried him through his trials.

Living in Hope

Living in hope requires us to focus on God's promises rather than our circumstances. Lamentations 3:21-23 teaches, "This I recall to my mind, therefore I have hope. Through the Lord's mercies we are not consumed, because His compassions fail not. They are new every morning; great is Your faithfulness." Remembering God's faithfulness fuels our hope.

Isaiah 40:31 encourages, "But those who wait on the Lord shall renew their strength; they shall mount up with wings like eagles, they shall run and not be weary, they shall walk and not faint." Hope gives us the strength to endure and the courage to trust God's timing.

Reflection Questions

How can you anchor your hope in God's promises rather than your circumstances?

_____

_____

_____

What are some ways you can share hope with others who may be struggling?

_____

_____

_____

How has God's faithfulness in the past strengthened your hope for the future?

_____

_____

_____

Prayer Prompt

Lord, thank You for being the source of my hope and strength. Teach me to trust in Your promises and to keep my eyes fixed on You, even in difficult times. Help me to share Your hope with others and to live with confidence in Your faithfulness. Amen.

Day 51: The Power of Faith

Faith as Our Foundation

Faith is the cornerstone of our relationship with God. Hebrews 11:1 defines faith as "the substance of things hoped for, the evidence of things not seen." Trusting in God allows us to step forward even when we don't have all the answers.

2 Corinthians 5:7 encourages, "For we walk by faith, not by sight." Faith invites us to rely on God's promises and His ability to guide us through every challenge.

Parable: The Blindfolded Walker

A guide led a blindfolded man through a dense forest. Each step felt uncertain, but the man trusted the guide's instructions, placing one foot in front of the other. When they reached a clearing, the man removed his blindfold to see a beautiful meadow.

The guide said, "Your trust brought you here, even when you couldn't see the way."

Faith is like walking blindfolded with God as our guide. Though we may not see the full path ahead, trusting Him allows us to reach destinations we could never imagine on our own.

Biblical Examples of Faith

The Bible is filled with stories of faith in action. Abraham demonstrated unwavering faith when he obeyed God's call to leave his homeland for an unknown destination (Genesis 12:1-4). His trust in God's promises made him the father of many nations.

Peter showed faith when he stepped out of the boat to walk on water toward Jesus. Though he faltered, his initial trust enabled him to experience the miraculous (Matthew 14:28-31). These stories remind us that faith empowers us to step into the unknown with confidence in God.

Growing in Faith

Faith grows as we trust God in both small and big moments. Romans 10:17 teaches, "So then faith comes by hearing, and hearing by the word of God." Spending time in Scripture strengthens our belief in His promises.

Faith also requires action. James 2:17 states, "Thus also faith by itself, if it does not have works, is dead." Trusting God inspires us to take steps that align with His plan, knowing He will provide what we need along the way.

Reflection Questions

What areas of your life require deeper faith in God's guidance?

_____

_____

_____

How has trusting God in the past strengthened your faith for current challenges?

_____

_____

_____

In what ways can you act on your faith to demonstrate your trust in God's promises?

_____

_____

_____

Prayer Prompt

Lord, thank You for being my guide and foundation of faith. Teach me to trust in Your promises and to take steps of obedience, even when the path is unclear. Help me to grow in faith and to live in a way that honors and glorifies You. Amen.

Day 52: The Power of Kindness

Kindness as a Reflection of God's Love

Kindness is a fruit of the Spirit that reflects God's love to the world. Ephesians 4:32 encourages, "And be kind to one another, tenderhearted, forgiving one another, even as God in Christ forgave you." Acts of kindness create opportunities to share God's grace and compassion.

Proverbs 19:17 reminds us, "He who has pity on the poor lends to the Lord, and He will pay back what he has given." Kindness is a way to serve God by serving others.

Parable: The Bread Giver

A baker noticed a hungry child lingering near his shop. Each day, he left a loaf of bread on the window ledge for the child to take. Years later, the baker fell ill and couldn't keep his business running. To his surprise, the now-grown child returned as a successful chef, bringing food to the baker daily.

The young chef said, "Your kindness fed me when I was in need; now I have the chance to repay it."

Kindness is like planting seeds—you may not see immediate results, but the harvest can grow in unexpected and beautiful ways.

Biblical Examples of Kindness

The Good Samaritan is a timeless example of kindness. While others passed by a man who had been beaten and left for dead, the Samaritan stopped, cared for his wounds, and ensured his safety (Luke 10:30-37).

His actions teach us that kindness transcends barriers and reflects God's heart.

Jesus also demonstrated kindness by healing the sick, feeding the hungry, and showing compassion to those in need. In Mark 6:34, Jesus saw the crowd and "was moved with compassion for them, because they were like sheep not having a shepherd." His kindness drew people closer to God's love.

Living a Life of Kindness

Kindness is an intentional choice that blesses both the giver and the receiver. Galatians 6:9-10 encourages, "And let us not grow weary while doing good, for in due season we shall reap if we do not lose heart. Therefore, as we have opportunity, let us do good to all, especially to those who are of the household of faith." Acts of kindness align us with God's purposes and bring joy to His heart.

Kindness also has the power to transform hearts. Romans 12:20-21 reminds us, "If your enemy is hungry, feed him; if he is thirsty, give him a drink...Do not be overcome by evil, but overcome evil with good." Responding with kindness can break down walls and create opportunities for reconciliation and peace.

Reflection Questions

How can you show kindness to someone in need this week?

_____

_____

_____

In what ways has God's kindness impacted your life and relationships?

_____

_____

_____

How can acts of kindness create opportunities to share God's love with others?

_____

_____

_____

Prayer Prompt

Lord, thank You for Your kindness and compassion in my life. Teach me to reflect Your love through acts of kindness, no matter how small or simple they may seem. Help me to see opportunities to serve others and to bring glory to Your name through my actions. Amen.

Day 53: The Gift of Patience

Patience as a Virtue

Patience is a vital fruit of the Spirit that allows us to endure challenges while trusting in God's timing. James 1:3-4 reminds us, "Knowing that the testing of your faith produces patience. But let patience have its perfect work, that you may be perfect and complete, lacking nothing." Through patience, God refines our character and strengthens our faith.

Romans 8:25 encourages, "But if we hope for what we do not see, we eagerly wait for it with perseverance." Trusting God's plan requires patience and faith in His perfect timing.

Parable: The Unripe Fruit

A farmer watched his son pluck an unripe apple from their orchard. The boy grimaced at the sour taste and asked, "Why doesn't it taste sweet?"

The farmer replied, "The fruit wasn't ready. If you'd waited, the sun would have ripened it, and it would have been perfect."

Patience is like waiting for fruit to ripen. Rushing ahead can lead to bitterness, but trusting in God's timing allows His blessings to develop fully, bringing joy and fulfillment.

Biblical Examples of Patience

The Bible highlights many individuals who demonstrated patience. Abraham and Sarah waited for decades for God's promise of a son. Their journey reminds us that God's timing is always best, even when it seems delayed (Genesis 21:1-2).

Job's story also illustrates the power of patience. Despite immense suffering, he declared, "Though He slay me, yet will I trust Him" (Job 13:15 NKJV). His unwavering patience and trust in God's sovereignty resulted in restoration and blessing.

Patience in Daily Life

Patience is not passive—it requires an active trust in God's plan. Psalm 27:14 encourages, "Wait on the Lord; be of good courage, and He shall strengthen your heart; wait, I say, on the Lord!" Choosing patience allows us to experience God's peace, even in the midst of uncertainty.

Colossians 3:12 urges, "Therefore, as God's chosen people, holy and dearly loved, clothe yourselves with compassion, kindness, humility, gentleness, and patience." Patience enables us to extend grace to others, fostering stronger relationships and reflecting God's love.

Reflection Questions

In what areas of your life do you need to practice more patience and trust in God's timing?

_____

_____

_____

How has waiting on God strengthened your character and faith?

_____

_____

_____

What steps can you take to develop greater patience in your interactions with others?

_____

_____

_____

Prayer Prompt

Lord, thank You for teaching me the value of patience. Help me to trust in Your timing and to wait with faith and courage. Teach me to extend patience and grace to others, reflecting Your love and kindness in my daily life. Amen.

Day 54: The Strength of Self-Control

Self-Control as a Fruit of the Spirit

Self-control is essential for living a life that honors God. Proverbs 25:28 warns, "Whoever has no rule over his own spirit is like a city broken down, without walls." Practicing self-control protects us from harm and aligns our lives with God's will.

Galatians 5:22-23 lists self-control as one of the fruits of the Spirit. It empowers us to resist temptation and make choices that glorify God.

Parable: The Wild Horse

A young man inherited a wild horse that ran wherever it pleased. No matter how hard he tried, he couldn't control it. Seeking advice, he asked an experienced trainer for help.

The trainer said, "With patience and discipline, you can teach the horse to obey."

Through consistent effort, the young man transformed the wild horse into a loyal companion, capable of great feats.

Self-control is like taming a wild horse. Without it, our impulses can lead us astray, but with God's guidance, we can channel our energy and desires toward His purpose.

Biblical Examples of Self-Control

Joseph exemplified self-control when he resisted the advances of Potiphar's wife. He declared, "How then can I do this great wickedness, and sin against God?" (Genesis 39:9 NKJV). His discipline preserved his integrity and positioned him for God's greater plan.

Daniel also showed self-control by refusing the king's rich food, choosing instead to honor God with his diet. His discipline resulted in God's favor and wisdom (Daniel 1:8-17). Both Joseph and Daniel remind us that self-control is rooted in a commitment to God's principles.

Living with Self-Control

Self-control requires us to submit our desires to God's will. 1 Corinthians 10:13 assures us, "No temptation has overtaken you except such as is common to man; but God is faithful, who will not allow you to be tempted beyond what you are able." Trusting God gives us the strength to overcome challenges.

Titus 2:11-12 encourages us, "For the grace of God that brings salvation has appeared to all men, teaching us that, denying ungodliness and worldly lusts, we should live soberly, righteously, and godly in the present age." Self-control allows us to live a life that reflects God's holiness.

Reflection Questions

In what areas of your life do you struggle with self-control, and how can you surrender those to God?

_____

_____

_____

How has practicing self-control helped you grow spiritually and strengthen your faith?

_____

_____

_____

What steps can you take to cultivate greater discipline and align your choices with God's will?

_____

_____

_____

Prayer Prompt

Lord, thank You for the gift of self-control through Your Spirit. Teach me to surrender my desires to You and to walk in obedience to Your will. Help me to practice discipline in every area of my life, reflecting Your holiness and love. Amen.

Day 55: The Power of Obedience

Obedience as an Act of Faith

Obedience to God is an expression of our trust and love for Him. John 14:15 says, "If you love Me, keep My commandments." Following God's instructions brings us closer to His purpose and allows His blessings to flow in our lives.

Deuteronomy 5:33 reminds us, "You shall walk in all the ways which the Lord your God has commanded you, that you may live and that it may be well with you." Obedience is the key to experiencing the fullness of God's promises.

Parable: The Builder's Blueprint

A builder received detailed blueprints for constructing a house. At first, he was tempted to take shortcuts, thinking, "No one will notice if I skip a few steps." But he chose to follow the plans exactly.

When a storm hit, the house stood firm, while others around it crumbled. The builder realized, "Obedience to the blueprint saved the house."

God's commands are like the blueprint for our lives. Following His guidance, even in the smallest details, ensures a strong foundation that can withstand life's challenges.

Biblical Examples of Obedience

Noah's obedience to God's instructions saved his family and preserved life on earth. Despite the ridicule of others, he followed God's commands to build the ark precisely as instructed (Genesis 6:22). His faith and obedience led to God's favor and protection.

Abraham also demonstrated obedience when God asked him to sacrifice Isaac. Though the request was incomprehensible, Abraham trusted God's plan. His obedience resulted in God providing a ram as a substitute and reaffirming His covenant (Genesis 22:1-18). These examples remind us that obedience often leads to greater blessings.

The Rewards of Obedience

Obedience brings blessings, protection, and a deeper relationship with God. Isaiah 1:19 promises, "If you are willing and obedient, you shall eat the good of the land." Trusting and following God's instructions lead to a life of abundance and purpose.

James 1:22 urges, "But be doers of the word, and not hearers only, deceiving yourselves." Obedience is not passive—it requires action and commitment to live out God's will daily.

Reflection Questions

What areas of your life require greater obedience to God's Word?

_____

_____

_____

How has obedience to God brought blessings or clarity to your life in the past?

_____

_____

_____

In what ways can you take intentional steps to align your actions with God's commands?

_____

_____

_____

Prayer Prompt

Lord, thank You for guiding me with Your Word and commandments. Teach me to trust and obey You in every area of my life. Help me to follow Your blueprint for my life with faith and commitment, knowing that Your plans are always for my good. Amen.

Day 56: The Power of Encouragement

Encouragement as a Ministry

Encouragement is a powerful way to uplift others and reflect God's love. 1 Thessalonians 5:11 reminds us, "Therefore comfort each other and edify one another, just as you also are doing." Speaking words of encouragement strengthens the faith and hope of those around us.

Proverbs 16:24 says, "Pleasant words are like a honeycomb, sweetness to the soul and health to the bones." Offering encouragement is not just an act of kindness but a ministry that brings healing and hope.

Parable: The Bridge Builder

A traveler reached a wide river and found no way to cross. Discouraged, he was about to turn back when an old man approached, saying, "Let's build a bridge together."

As they worked side by side, the traveler found new strength. When the bridge was complete, he realized the old man had helped him not only cross the river but also regain his courage for the journey ahead.

Encouragement is like building a bridge—it helps others move forward when they feel stuck. By offering support and guidance, we reflect God's strength and love.

Biblical Examples of Encouragement

Barnabas, whose name means "Son of Encouragement," played a vital role in the early church. He supported Paul when others doubted him and encouraged the believers to remain faithful (Acts 11:22-24). His example teaches us the importance of building others up in their faith.

Jesus also encouraged His disciples, reminding them of God's faithfulness and power. In John 16:33, He said, "These things I have spoken to you, that in Me you may have peace. In the world you will have tribulation; but be of good cheer, I have overcome the world." His words gave them courage to face challenges with confidence.

Living a Life of Encouragement

Encouragement is a daily practice that transforms relationships and communities. Hebrews 10:24-25 urges, "And let us consider one another in order to stir up love and good works, not forsaking the assembling of ourselves together...but exhorting one another." Supporting others strengthens the body of Christ and fosters unity.

Colossians 4:6 reminds us, "Let your speech always be with grace, seasoned with salt, that you may know how you ought to answer each one." Speaking words of grace and encouragement brings light to others and glorifies God.

Reflection Questions

Who in your life could use encouragement today, and how can you support them?

_____

_____

_____

How has someone else's encouragement strengthened your faith and confidence?

_____

_____

_____

What steps can you take to make encouragement a regular part of your interactions with others?

_____

_____

_____

Prayer Prompt

Lord, thank You for the gift of encouragement and the opportunity to build others up. Teach me to speak words of hope and faith, reflecting Your love in all that I say and do. Help me to strengthen those around me and to be a source of light and encouragement in their lives. Amen.

Day 57: Replenished Through Serving

Serving as a Reflection of God's Love

Serving others is a powerful way to express God's love and fulfill His purpose. Galatians 5:13 encourages, "For you, brethren, have been called to liberty; only do not use liberty as an opportunity for the flesh, but through love serve one another." Service transforms our faith into action and blesses both the giver and the receiver.

Mark 10:45 reminds us, "For even the Son of Man did not come to be served, but to serve, and to give His life a ransom for many." Jesus' life of service is the ultimate example of selfless love.

Parable: The Overflowing Well

A village suffered from a long drought, and the people grew weary searching for water. One man, who owned a deep well, freely offered water to anyone in need. When asked why he didn't keep it for himself, he replied, "The more I draw from the well, the more it fills."

His generosity inspired others to share what little they had, and the village thrived despite the drought.

Service is like drawing from a well—when we give to others, God replenishes our strength and resources, allowing us to continue serving with joy.

Biblical Examples of Service

Jesus exemplified servanthood when He washed His disciples' feet, saying, "If I then, your Lord and Teacher, have washed your feet, you also ought to wash one another's feet" (John 13:14 NKJV). His act of humility teaches us that no task is too small or unimportant when done in love.

The Good Samaritan also demonstrated the heart of a servant by caring for a wounded man. He not only provided immediate aid but ensured the man's recovery, going above and beyond what was expected (Luke 10:30-37). His actions reflect the sacrificial nature of true service.

The Blessings of Serving

Serving others brings joy, purpose, and fulfillment. Proverbs 11:25 declares, "The generous soul will be made rich, and he who waters will also be watered himself." When we serve with a willing heart, God blesses our efforts and strengthens our faith.

Matthew 25:40 reminds us that serving others is a way of serving God: "Assuredly, I say to you, inasmuch as you did it to one of the least of these My brethren, you did it to Me." Every act of service, no matter how small, has eternal significance.

Reflection Questions

How can you use your time, talents, and resources to serve others in your community?

_____

_____

_____

In what ways has serving others deepened your relationship with God?

_____

_____

_____

How can you cultivate a heart of service in your daily life?

_____

_____

_____

Prayer Prompt

Lord, thank You for the privilege of serving others and reflecting Your love. Teach me to serve with humility, joy, and a willing heart. Help me to see opportunities to bless those around me and to glorify You through every act of service. Amen.

Day 58: The Gift of Generational Legacy

Building a Legacy That Honors God

A generational legacy is about passing down faith, values, and wisdom to those who come after us. Psalm 78:4 reminds us, "We will not hide them from their children, telling to the generation to come the praises of the Lord, and His strength and His wonderful works that He has done." Leaving a legacy rooted in God's truth ensures that His faithfulness endures through the ages.

Proverbs 13:22 declares, "A good man leaves an inheritance to his children's children." Our actions today shape the spiritual and moral foundation for future generations.

Parable: The Great Oak

A man planted an oak tree in his field, knowing he would never see its full height. When his grandson asked why he was planting it, he replied, "This tree isn't for me—it's for you and those who will come after you. Its shade will protect you, and its wood will build your home."

Years later, the grandson marveled at the towering oak, realizing the sacrifice and foresight it took to plant something for the benefit of others.

A legacy is like the oak tree—it takes time to grow, but its blessings extend far beyond the planter's lifetime.

Biblical Examples of Legacy

Abraham's faith and obedience established a covenant that extended to his descendants, making him the father of many nations (Genesis 17:7). His trust in God created a foundation for future generations to walk in faith.

Timothy's legacy of faith began with his grandmother Lois and his mother Eunice. Paul commended their influence, saying, "I call to remembrance the genuine faith that is in you, which dwelt first in your grandmother Lois and your mother Eunice" (2 Timothy 1:5 NKJV). Their spiritual legacy shaped Timothy's life and ministry.

Living for a Lasting Legacy

Creating a legacy requires intentionality. Deuteronomy 6:6-7 encourages, "And these words which I command you today shall be in your heart. You shall teach them diligently to your children." Passing down God's truths and values ensures that they remain central to future generations.

A legacy also involves living as an example. Matthew 5:16 reminds us, "Let your light so shine before men, that they may see your good works and glorify your Father in heaven." Our actions today can inspire others to live lives of faith, love, and purpose.

Reflection Questions

What values and truths do you want to pass on to the next generation?

_____

_____

_____

How can you be intentional about building a God-honoring legacy in your family or community?

_____

_____

_____

What steps can you take today to invest in the spiritual growth of those around you?

_____

_____

_____

Prayer Prompt

Lord, thank You for the opportunity to build a legacy that honors You. Teach me to live with intention and to pass on faith, wisdom, and love to the next generation. Help me to be a light and an example, inspiring others to follow You and glorify Your name. Amen.

Day 59: The Power of Vision

Seeing Through God's Eyes

Vision is the ability to see beyond the present and align ourselves with God's plans. Proverbs 29:18 reminds us, "Where there is no vision, the people perish: but he that keepeth the law, happy is he." God's vision provides direction, purpose, and clarity for our lives.

Habakkuk 2:2 encourages, "Write the vision and make it plain on tablets, that he may run who reads it." Embracing God's vision inspires action and perseverance, even in challenging times.

Parable: The Mountain Climber

A climber set out to reach the peak of a mountain. Halfway up, fog rolled in, obscuring his view. Discouraged, he considered turning back, but his guide urged him to press on. "The summit is closer than it seems," the guide said.

When they broke through the fog, the climber saw the breathtaking peak, realizing the guide had seen it all along.

Vision is like climbing through the fog—though we may not see the outcome, trusting God as our guide leads us to heights we could never reach on our own.

Biblical Examples of Vision

Nehemiah had a clear vision to rebuild the walls of Jerusalem. Despite opposition, he rallied the people and completed the task, saying, "The God of heaven Himself will prosper us; therefore we His servants will arise and build" (Nehemiah 2:20 NKJV). His vision inspired action and unity.

Jesus, too, lived with vision. He came to seek and save the lost, declaring, "For the Son of Man has come to seek and to save that which was lost" (Luke 19:10 NKJV). His vision of redemption shaped His ministry and brought salvation to the world.

Living with Vision

Living with vision means seeking God's direction and stepping forward in faith. Isaiah 30:21 promises, "Your ears shall hear a word behind you, saying, 'This is the way, walk in it.'" Trusting God's guidance allows us to stay on the path He has prepared.

Vision also requires perseverance. Hebrews 12:1-2 urges, "Let us run with endurance the race that is set before us, looking unto Jesus, the author and finisher of our faith." Keeping our eyes on God's purpose empowers us to overcome obstacles and fulfill His plan.

Reflection Questions

What vision has God placed on your heart, and how can you take steps to pursue it?

_____

_____

_____

How can you trust God's guidance when the path ahead feels uncertain?

_____

_____

_____

In what ways can you align your daily actions with the vision God has for your life?

_____

_____

_____

Prayer Prompt

Lord, thank You for giving me a vision and a purpose for my life. Teach me to trust Your guidance, even when the path is unclear. Help me to live with faith, perseverance, and clarity, knowing that You are leading me toward Your perfect plan. Amen.

Day 60: The Journey of Faith

Walking by Faith, Not by Sight

Faith is a lifelong journey of trusting God, even when the path is unclear. 2 Corinthians 5:7 reminds us, "For we walk by faith, not by sight." Each step we take in obedience brings us closer to the fulfillment of God's promises.

Hebrews 11:6 teaches, "But without faith it is impossible to please Him, for he who comes to God must believe that He is, and that He is a rewarder of those who diligently seek Him." Faith requires us to trust in God's character and His faithfulness to guide us.

Parable: The Lantern in the Darkness

A traveler set out on a journey through the forest at night, carrying only a small lantern. The light illuminated just enough of the path for him to take one step at a time. Though he couldn't see the destination, he trusted the lantern to guide him safely.

When he reached his goal, he realized the journey had strengthened his trust and taught him patience.

Faith is like the traveler's lantern—it may not reveal the whole path, but it provides enough light for each step. Trusting God day by day leads us to His perfect plan.

Biblical Examples of Faith Journeys

Abraham's journey of faith began when God called him to leave his homeland for an unknown destination. Genesis 12:1 records God's command: "Get out of your country, from your family and from your father's house, to a land that I will show you." Abraham's obedience, despite uncertainty, established him as the father of faith.

The Israelites' exodus from Egypt also reflects a journey of faith. Led by Moses, they followed God's guidance through the wilderness, trusting Him to provide manna, water, and protection. Their story reminds us that faith often requires endurance and trust in God's timing.

Faith in the Present and Future

Faith is not just about the destination—it's about the process. James 1:3-4 encourages, "Knowing that the testing of your faith produces patience. But let patience have its perfect work, that you may be perfect and complete, lacking nothing." Challenges along the way refine our character and deepen our reliance on God.

Philippians 1:6 assures us, "Being confident of this very thing, that He who has begun a good work in you will complete it until the day of Jesus Christ." Trusting God to finish what He started brings peace and hope as we continue our journey.

Reflection Questions

How has your faith journey strengthened your trust in God?

_____
_____
_____

What challenges are you facing that require you to walk by faith?

_____
_____
_____

How can you encourage others in their journeys of faith, reminding them of God's promises?

_____
_____
_____

Prayer Prompt

Lord, thank You for walking with me on this journey of faith. Teach me to trust You step by step, even when the path is unclear. Help me to encourage others and to remain steadfast, knowing that You are guiding me toward Your perfect plan. Amen.

Acknowledgments

First and foremost, I give all glory to God for the vision, strength, and grace to complete this devotional. What began as a seed of inspiration has now become a resource, I pray will impact lives around the world.

To my wife, Laquvia Garrett, thank you for your unwavering love, encouragement, and prayers. Your strength, wisdom, and heart for God continue to inspire me every day. This journey would not be the same without your support and faith beside me.

To my parents, Richard and Renita Garrett, thank you for being the foundation of faith, integrity, and perseverance in my life. Your example shaped me and your belief in me sustained me.

To my sister, Ruby Garrett, thank you for your consistent love, laughter, and encouragement. You've always been in my corner, and I'm forever grateful.

To Pastor Tommy Vallejos, Pastor Anthony Daley, and Pastor Keith Battle, thank you for being spiritual mentors, teachers, and examples of servant leadership. Your lives, ministries, and messages helped fuel the spiritual depth of this work.

To everyone who has supported, prayed, and believed in the message behind Created to Believe—thank you. This devotional is a reflection of not just my journey, but of every person who has ever dared to trust God's process.

With love and gratitude,
Richard "Reason" Garrett

About the Author

Richard "Reason" Garrett is a devoted husband, father, entrepreneur, and servant-leader whose life and work reflect a deep commitment to purpose, community, and faith. With a background as a United States Marine, civic leader, and real estate broker, Richard brings a unique blend of discipline, wisdom, and heart to everything he does.

A former Clarksville City Councilman, Mayor Pro Tem (Vice Mayor), and Commissioner on the Regional Planning Commission, Richard has championed policies that empower underserved communities and fuel regional growth. His leadership has left a lasting impact on the city he calls home.

As the Owner and Principal Broker of Concord Realty, Richard is known for his tenacity, fairness, and integrity. With more than a decade of success in real estate, he's guided countless families, especially military and first-time homebuyers, toward stability, homeownership, and financial empowerment.

A visionary at heart, Richard is also the founder of **Liberated Publishing, Inc.** and the **LEAP Organization**, a nonprofit that has provided mentorship, housing, and entrepreneurial training for over 1,200 youth and single-parent households. Under his leadership, LEAP transformed a 24,000-square-foot facility into the **Clarksville Entrepreneur Center**, a beacon of opportunity for the next generation of leaders and innovators.

Richard holds a Bachelor's degree in Public Management from Austin Peay State University and is a proud product of Clarksville, Tennessee. His life's journey from El Paso to the Marine Corps, from city council chambers to business boardrooms—has been shaped by faith, fortified by resilience, and fueled by a relentless belief in purpose.

Created to Believe: 60 Days of Faith, Strength, and Purpose reflects that belief. It's more than a book, it's a movement to remind readers that no matter where they start, they were created with divine intention.

To connect with Richard, explore speaking opportunities, or learn more about his work, visit:

🔎 https://www.unleashedlc.com/consulting
✉ reason1041@gmail.com

www.ingramcontent.com/pod-product-compliance
Lightning Source LLC
Chambersburg PA
CBHW020924090426
42736CB00010B/1029